True Eskimo Stories of Ghosts and Evil Spirits

by the
Grandson of a Good Shaman

Bloomington, IN  Milton Keynes, UK

authorHOUSE®

AuthorHouse™
1663 Liberty Drive, Suite 200
Bloomington, IN 47403
www.authorhouse.com
Phone: 1-800-839-8640

AuthorHouse™ UK Ltd.
500 Avebury Boulevard
Central Milton Keynes, MK9 2BE
www.authorhouse.co.uk
Phone: 08001974150

First published by AuthorHouse 11/20/2006

ISBN: 978-1-4259-7338-4 (sc)

Printed in the United States of America
Bloomington, Indiana

This book is printed on acid-free paper.

THE STORIES

TOO LATE

THIS POOR OLD WOMAN'S BAD ENDING, FOR A VERY TERRIBLE BAD MISTAKE WHILE SHE WAS YET STILL ALIVE AND WELL, CAME AT THE CLOSING ENDING OF HER GIFT OF DAILY LIFE. HERE, ON THIS SOMEWHAT GOOD PLACE, IN WHICH WE ALL LIVE, CALLED AND KNOWN AS THE EARTH, WHILE THIS WOMAN IN QUESTION WAS YET ALIVE AND WELL, SHE CHOSE TO BE A VERY BAD SOUL. FOR WHENEVER SHE MET ANY OF THE OTHER LIVING SOULS LIVING IN HER HOME VILLAGE, SHE MADE SURE TO LET IT BE KNOWN TO THEM THAT SHE, THE BAD WOMAN SOUL, DID NOT EVEN LIKE THEM ONE BIT, LET ALONE CARE ABOUT THEM. ALL IN ALL, WHEN SHE WAS AROUND AND ABOUT HER HOME VILLAGE, SHE SENSELESSLY CALLED THEM BAD NAMES AND WAS VERY FOND OF PUTTING THEM DOWN, SO THAT THEY WOULD FEEL BAD, SEEM TO BE WORTHLESS, AND OTHER BAD STUFF ASSOCIATED WITH THE SENSIBLE GIFT OF THEIR DAILY LIVES THAT THEY WERE EXISTING IN, IN THAT PARTICULAR TIME FRAME. SO, ALL THE OTHER VILLAGERS TRIED THEIR BEST. THEY KNEW HOW TO KEEP OUT OF HER WAY WHENEVER THEY HAPPENED TO SEE HER COMING THEIR

WAY. THEY ALWAYS CHOSE TO GO OTHER WAYS OR STEP ASIDE, SO THEY WOULD NOT MEET HER HEAD-ON. SHE WAS LIVING HER BAD MISTAKE DURING HER LIFETIME, EVER SINCE SHE WAS QUITE A VERY YOUNG AGE, IN FACT. AND SHE DID LIVE TO A VERY RIPE OLD AGE, SO IT WAS QUITE A SPELL THAT SHE WAS IN HER CHOSEN BAD CONDITION, UNTIL SHE GOT QUITE OLD. BUT THE BAD WAS TO BE PAID BACK IN FULL, DURING THE COURSE OF HER ENDING GIFT OF HER DAILY BREATH. ON HER DEATHBED, SHE DID FIND OUT THE HARD WAY THAT ALL HER SINS WERE TO BE PAID BY HER SOUL, WHICH WILL NEVER DIE, EVEN IF THE BODY DIES. SHE STARTED TO WITHER AND KEPT ASKING FOR WATER FROM OTHERS THAT WERE WITH HER. ONE OF THEM HAPPENED TO ASK HER WHAT THE MATTER WAS, AND SHE, THE BAD SOUL, TOLD THEM THAT A VERY HOT FIRE WAS COMING CLOSER AND CLOSER TOWARDS HER, FROM BELOW HER, AND SHE ALSO STATED THAT THE DEVIL'S FOUL-SMELLING AND UGLY, EVIL-LOOKING DEMONS WERE GETTING READY TO TAKE HER VERY SOUL INTO HELL, WHERE SHE WOULD BE TORTURED BY THEM, BY FIRE AND OTHER PAINFUL THINGS, EXECUTED BY THE EVIL DEMONS WITH VERY FOUL ODORS COMING FROM THEIR SHAPES AND FORMS. SHE WAS CRYING REALLY LOUDLY, AND WITHERING AND SCREAMING VERY LOUDLY JUST BEFORE HER DEATH. THE PEOPLE THAT

WERE WITNESSING THIS BAD ENDING OF THIS FORMER BAD SOUL WERE VERY SCARED OF WHAT WAS TAKING PLACE AT THE TIME OF THIS BAD WOMAN SOUL'S DEATHBED.

DEMON'S VISIT

LATE ONE COLD, MOONLESS EVENING, A VERY STRONG MAN WAS GOING ABOUT GETTING HIMSELF PREPARED FOR HIS VERY MUCH NEEDED EVENING MEAL, SO THAT HIS STRENGTH WOULD CONTINUE, AND SO THAT HE HIMSELF WOULD WITHOUT A DOUBT CONTINUE IN HIS STRONG MAN WAYS. AT ABOUT MIDWAY, AS HE WENT ABOUT HIS MEAL FOR THIS EVENING'S CONSUMPTION OF HIS DAILY FOOD INTAKE, HE HAPPENED TO HEAR A KNOCK ON HIS MOOSE HIDE DOORWAY. HE WAS SURPRISED, SINCE HE DID NOT GET MANY VISITORS TO HIS HUT, WHICH HE HAD LIVED IN FOR QUITE SOME TIME. HE THEREFORE WENT TO CHECK OUT WHO IN THE WORLD WAS MAKING THAT KNOCK ON HIS SOMEWHAT OLD MOOSE HIDE DOORWAY. WHEN HE OPENED HIS DOOR, HE SAW THAT IT WAS A VERY TALL AND EVIL-FACED DEMON--NOT TO MENTION HIS SMELL, WHICH WAS VERY FOUL AND REALLY STUNK--ONE OF THE FALLEN ANGELS. BUT NOW, IT WAS AN UGLY, FOUL-SMELLING EVIL DEMON, A SERVANT OF THE EVIL ONE HIMSELF. ALL THE TALL AND EVIL DEMON SAID TO HIM THAT FIRST EVENING WAS THIS QUOTE: "I HAVE COME."

AND NOTHING FURTHER WAS SAID BY THE FOUL-SMELLING ONE. ON THE SECOND DAY, THIS STRONG MAN IN QUESTION HAPPENED TO HEAR ANOTHER KNOCK ON HIS DOOR. HE WAS NOT TOO SURPRISED THIS TIME AROUND, AND SAW WHAT HE EXPECTED TO SEE. THAT WAS THAT SAME FOUL-SMELLING, TALL, AND UGLY ONE HIMSELF--THE EVIL DEMON, THAT IS. THIS TIME AROUND, WHAT CAME OUT OF HIS MULTI-TOOTHED MOUTH MADE A LITTLE MORE SENSE TO THE STRONG ONE HIMSELF. WHAT HE SAID WAS THIS: "I HAVE COME TO CLAIM YOUR." AND AGAIN, NOTHING FURTHER WAS SAID BY THIS FOUL-SMELLING UGLY OLD DEMON. SO THEN AGAIN, HE SHUT HIS DOORWAY'S FLAP. ON THE THIRD DAY, AFTER MUCH THINKING, THE STRONG ONE HIMSELF KNEW THAT IF HE JUST SO MUCH AS ALLOWED THE EVIL DEMON TO FINISH HIS SENTENCE, HE WOULD NO LONGER BE ALIVE. SO HE PREPARED HIS FIREPLACE, AND MADE SURE THAT THERE WOULD BE ENOUGH HOT COALS FOR HIM TO SPLASH THE OLD FOUL ODOR, AND TEACH HIM A THING OR TWO. SURE ENOUGH, THE THIRD EVENING ROLLED AROUND WITH THAT SAME OLD DOORWAY KNOCK. AS SOON AS HE HEARD THE KNOCK, THE TOUGH GUY FILLED A WOODEN BOWL WITH THOSE HOT COALS, RAN TO HIS DOORWAY, AND SPLASHED THE ODOR-FILLED TALL AND DARK ONE WITH THOSE HOT COALS, WHICH WERE VERY HOT. AS SOON AS THE HOT COALS HIT THE TALL

AND DARK SMELLY ONE, HE CAUGHT ON FIRE AND DISAPPEARED INTO THE GROUND, SWEARING AND SCREAMING ALL THE WHILE. HE WAS NEVER TO BE SEEN BY THIS STRONG MAN EVER AGAIN. HE KNEW THAT THE EVIL DEMON WAS AFTER HIS SOUL, TO CLAIM IT FOR HIS MASTER, THE DEVIL, THE FATHER OF ALL EVIL THINGS.

THE ONE AND ONLY

THIS GOOD OLD GAL WOULD OFTEN VENTURE WITHIN HER HOME VILLAGE AND THIS GAL SOUL HUMAN WOULD OFTEN WALK ABOUT HER BIRTHPLACE, LOOKING FOR ANY MAN TO BE HER VERY OWN. BUT MUCH TO HER DISMAY AND BAD LUCK, SHE COULD NOT HITCH UP WITH SOUL MAN BROTHERS WHO KNEW THAT SHE WAS WEIRD AND LOOKED UGLY, SO UGLY. SO THEY KEPT REFUSING TO BE HER HUSBAND AND PARTNER. THIS KEPT ON FOR A LONG TIME. AND STILL THE MEN KEPT REFUSING HER, DESPITE HER ONGOING EFFORTS, UNTIL ONE FATED DAY, WHEN SHE MADE A MISTAKE. SHE HELD HER NOSE HIGH UP IN THE AIR. BY HER VERY OWN HARD-HEADED NATURE, SHE WENT AROUND AND ACTED AS IF SHE WAS ABOVE EVERYONE ELSE. WHENEVER ANYONE WAS STANDING IN HER WAY, SHE WOULD MATTER-OF-FACTLY SAY, "OUT OF MY WAY," WITH A VERY DIFFERENT ATTITUDE THAT SHE HAD NOT HAD IN HER PAST, BEFORE HER SUDDEN CHANGE INTO A NEW PERSON. ALL OF THIS SOUL SISTER'S ACTIONS WOULD ONE DAY BE A CAUSE OF TROUBLE FOR HER. THIS WENT ON FOR ABOUT A MONTH OR SO, WHEN ONE LATE

EVENING SHE WAS RETURNING HOME FROM A CHURCH SERVICE. SHE WAS ABOUT TO SEE A NOT-SO-FRIENDLY GHOST. WHEN SHE GOT TO HER PORCH, SHE SAW SOMEONE THAT WAS GOING AGAINST HER LAW OF BEING IN HER WAY. AFTER SAYING "OUT OF MY WAY," WHEN THE THING STILL WOULD NOT MOVE OUT OF HER WAY AS SHE HAD REQUESTED, SHE MADE HER WRONG MOVE. SHE WAS ABOUT TO PUSH THE COLD-FEELING THING OUT OF HER WAY. SHE FOUND OUT THAT SHE COULD NOT EVEN MOVE HIM AN INCH. THEN SHE REALIZED THAT IT WAS A NON-LIVING ONE. SHE THEN STARTED SLOWLY BACKING OFF, ALL THE WHILE LOOKING UGLIER THAN SHE HAD EVER LOOKED DURING HER ENTIRE LIFE. THAT WAS AFTER SEEING THAT THING SHE JUST SAW WAS A RECENTLY DEARLY DEPARTED ONE, ONE OF THOSE TO WHOM SHE HAD OFTEN QUOTED HER MUCH-USED WHOLE SENTENCE, "OUT OF MY WAY." AFTER BACKING OFF REALLY SLOWLY, SHE RAN TO ANOTHER PERSON'S HOUSE AND SPENT HER NIGHT WITH THEM. NO, SHE DID NOT SUDDENLY TURN INTO A PRINCESS, BUT WAS NOW A MUCH BETTER PERSON, AND STARTED BEING GOOD TO EVERYONE IN HER HOMETOWN. THAT WAS DUE TO SEEING SOMETHING THAT SHE HAD NEVER, EVER SEEN IN HER ENTIRE LIFETIME ON OUR GOOD PLACE, THE EARTH.

SAVED BY AN ANGEL

THERE WAS A VERY GOOD-HEARTED WOMAN WHO, BY HER OWN CHOICE, MADE HERSELF KNOWN AS A PERSON WHO LOVED TO HELP OTHERS, ESPECIALLY THE ELDERLY OF HER HOME VILLAGE. THIS GOOD SOUL, WHO WAS VERY MUCH APPRECIATED BY HER FELLOW VILLAGERS, HAPPENED TO BE OUT FROM HER VILLAGE TO GATHER SOME PLANTS, WHICH WERE USED FOR MEDICAL CURES BY THE ELDERLY THAT SHE OFTEN HELPED OUT WITH CHORES THAT WERE NOT ON SHORT SUPPLY, BUT WERE REQUIRED TO BE TAKEN CARE OF ON A DAILY BASIS. SHE WAS OUT IN HER WILDERNESS, VENTURING AWAY FROM HOME, WHEN SHE DECIDED TO WALK ON THE NEWLY FROZEN RIVER, THINKING THAT MAY MAKE HER WALK ON A MUCH BETTER TRAIL. AS SHE WAS ON HER WAY ON THE ICE WALK, SHE GOT INTO A LITTLE PROBLEM, WHICH SHE, BY HER OWN POWER, WOULD NOT BE ABLE TO TAKE CARE OF, LET ALONE GET OUT OF. SHE WAS DOING HER WALK ON A MUCH BETTER TRAIL, WHEN SHE HAPPENED TO FALL INTO THE WATER BENEATH THE FROZEN ICE. BUT LUCK WAS WITH HER, AND SHE WAS ABLE TO TOUCH THE BOTTOM OF THE RIVER, BUT

MUCH LIKE HER CURRENT LUCK SO FAR, GOT LODGED IN THE HOLE THAT SHE HAD FALLEN THROUGH. SHE DID TRY HER BEST TO CLIMB UP AND OUT OF THE HOLE, BUT FOUND OUT THAT SHE COULD NOT GET HERSELF OUT BY HER OWN POWER. THERE WAS NO ONE AROUND HER AREA TO HELP HER GET OUT OF HER CURRENT SITUATION. WHEN, AFTER MANY TRIES, SHE WAS ABOUT TO GIVE UP, SHE HAPPENED TO LOOK UP INTO THE SKY AND SAW A TINY SPECK OF BRIGHT LIGHT COMING DOWN TOWARDS HER PLACE OF TROUBLE. AS SHE WATCHED THIS UNIDENTIFIED SOMETHING, IT CAME CLOSER AND CLOSER. THEN SHE REALIZED THAT IT WAS A MAN WITH REALLY NICE-LOOKING CLOTHES, WHICH SHE, THE GOOD WOMAN SOUL HAD NEVER HAD, NOT TO MENTION SEEN, BEFORE. THEN, MUCH TO HER SURPRISE, HE HELPED HER GET OUT OF HER CURRENT SITUATION. WHEN SHE TRIED TO THANK HIM, HE WOULD NOT LET HER DO SO, BUT RATHER, TOLD HER THIS: "YOU HAVE MANY MORE YEARS TO DO YOUR GOOD WORKS, TO HELP OUT THOSE IN NEED OF YOUR SERVICES DAILY." AFTER SAYING THIS, THE ANGEL AGAIN STARTED ASCENDING UP INTO THE HEAVENS. WHEN HE WAS FINALLY OUT OF HER SIGHT, SHE PROCEEDED TO GET HERSELF DRIED OFF. AFTER BUILDING A SMALL FIRE TO DO SO, THIS TIME AROUND, SHE TOOK ANOTHER TRAIL BACK TO HER HOME VILLAGE ON SOLID GROUND, WITH THE

CURING MEDICINE PLANTS THAT SHE KNEW
WERE MUCH NEEDED BY THOSE THAT WERE
NOT ABLE TO DO FOR THEMSELVES.

LED BY SATAN

THESE CARD-PLAYING LIVING SOULS WERE ON THEIR FAVORITE PASTIME, AND THAT WAS TO WIN SOME MONEY FROM THE OTHER SOULS THAT WERE PRESENT, ALSO TRYING TO DO THE SAME. ONE OF THESE, MAYBE TWO, HAD MADE A TRIP INTO TOWN TO PICK UP SOME ILLEGAL BEVERAGES FOR THEM TO HAVE A GOOD TIME, ALSO. DURING THEIR GAMING ACTIVITIES, ONE POOR OLD SOUL WAS NOT HAVING MUCH LUCK WHILE HE WAS INVOLVED FULLY. THIS CARD-LOSING SOUL WAS TAKING MORE THAN HE COULD HANDLE, OR THE TRUTH WAS, HE WAS DRINKING MORE THAN THE OTHERS PRESENT WITH MINDS OF THEIR OWN. AFTER HE HAD LOST ALL HIS MONEY, HE TOLD THE OTHERS THAT HE WAS GOING HOME, BACK TO HIS HOUSE. THERE WAS A FULL MOON, AND THE LATE NIGHT TEMPERATURE WAS QUITE COLD. AS HE WAS HEADING BACK, THESE OTHER TWO SOULS THAT HAD ALSO HELPED TO RIP OFF HIS HARD-EARNED MONEY WERE OUT ON THE PORCH HAVING A SMOKE BREAK. THEN, WHEN THEY REALIZED THAT THE LOSER THAT WAS ON HIS WAY HOME WAS GOING TOWARDS THE LOCAL CEMETARY, AWAY

FROM HIS HOUSE, THEY GOT CONCERNED FOR HIS SAFTY, AND ONE OF THEM WENT AFTER HIM TO SEE FOR WHAT REASON OR REASONS HE WAS HEADNG TOWARD THE PLACEMENT AREA OF FORMERLY LIVING SOULS--DEAD BODIES. WHEN THIS OTHER SOUL CAUGHT UP WITH THE LOSER SOUL, HE FOUND HIM WEARING ONLY HIS T-SHIRT, SO HE PICKED HIM UP SO THAT HE WOULD NOT FREEZE TO DEATH OUTSIDE, WHICH WAS QUITE COLD, AND BROUGHT HIM BACK TO HIS HOME. WHEN THE MAN WHO HAD SAVED HIM ASKED HIM QUESTIONS ABOUT HIS REASON FOR HEADING TOWARDS THE LOCAL CEMETARY, HE THEN LET IT ALL OUT. HE TOLD HIM THAT THE EVIL ONE HIMSELF WAS LEADING THE WAY, AND THAT WHENEVER THE EVIL DEVIL TOLD HIM TO REMOVE THE ARTICLES OF CLOTHING HE WAS WEARING, HE DID SO. HE TOLD HIM THAT HE WAS ALSO POWERLESS TO REFUSE WHAT SATAN HAD STATED FOR HIM TO DO, AND THAT HE WAS DOING SO AGAINST HIS WILL, DUE TO NOT HAVING ANY POWER TO FIGHT BACK. THAT WAS WHAT THE CAUSE WAS, HE SAID. BUT THANKS TO HIS CARD-PLAYING BUDDY'S CONCERN FOR HIS SAFETY, HIS LIFE WAS SPARED FROM BEING TAKEN BY THE DEVIL, WHO WITHOUT A DOUBT WAS AFTER HIS SOUL. FOR HE HIMSELF, THE EVIL ONE, SATAN, COULD TAKE HIS SOUL AND TORTURE HIM WITH FIRE AND OTHER TORTURE METHODS, WHICH HE CARRIES OUT FOR LOST SOULS,

WHO, AT THIS VERY MOMENT, DO NOT BELIEVE OR HAD OFTEN THOUGHT THAT HE IS NOT SUCH A BAD FALLEN ANGEL. BUT HE IS MUCH MORE EVIL THAN WHAT PEOPLE THINK OF HIM UP TO THIS VERY DAY. BUT IT WILL END SOMEDAY, WHEN GOD THROWS HIM INTO FIRE BURNING WITH BRIMSTONE, AND STRIPS HIM OF ALL HIS POWERS BEFORE DOING SO.

LITTLE MAN ELF IMP

A WOMAN WAS OUT PICKING BERRIES, OUT AWAY FROM HER HOME VILLAGE, AND THIS VERY ALIVE SOUL WAS QUITE A DISTANCE AWAY FROM IT ALL. SHE WAS DOING QUITE WELL WITH HER BERRY-PICKING, ABOUT WHICH SHE HAD A VERY CLEAR CONSCIENCE THAT ALL THE TASTY FRESH BERRIES WOULD BE PUT TO GOOD USE BY HER AS DESSERT FOODS THAT SHE COULD MAKE. SHE WAS OUT FOR THE BETTER PART OF THAT DAY, AND WAS PRETTY MUCH SATISFIED WITH ALL THE BERRIES THAT SHE HAD PICKED UP, FOR SHE HAD BEEN HARD AT WORK BY HERSELF, SINCE SHE HAD A REALLY BIG PROBLEM: NOT BEING ABLE TO CONCEIVE, TO HAVE CHILDREN WITH HER CURRENT HUSBAND. NOT A SINGLE ORPHAN WAS AVAILABLE FOR THEM TO ADOPT, TO CALL THEIR VERY OWN CHILD. THIS WAS DUE TO THE FACT THAT THESE WERE TIMES OF PLENTY, AND ALL WAS GOING WELL FOR ALL THE OTHER LIVING SOULS BACK IN HER HOME VILLAGE. WHILE HARD AT WORK, PICKING THOSE BERRIES, ALL SORTS OF THOUGHTS WERE THOUGHT OUT BY THIS WOMAN, WHO COULD NOT GET WHAT SHE WAS HOPING FOR, AND HAD LONGED FOR

EVER SINCE THE VERY FIRST DAY THAT SHE HAD GOTTEN HITCHED UP TO HER CURRENT HUSBAND. SHE ALSO KNEW THAT WAS NOT DUE TO ANY CURSE OR HEX THAT WAS THE CAUSE OF HER CONDITION, FOR SHE WAS AT PEACE WITH ALL OF THE OTHERS BACK HOME. SHE WAS FEELING REALLY LOW AND QUITE DEPRESSED, WHEN SHE THEREFORE DECIDED FOR HERSELF THAT SHE WOULD HAVE HER MUCH NEEDED LUNCH. WHEN SHE SAT DOWN TO ENJOY HER MEAL, ALL OF HER EMOTIONS SUDDENLY OVERCAME HER AND SHE STARTED TO CRY OUT UNCONTROLLABLY AND REALLY LOUDLY, SINCE SHE KNEW THAT NO ONE WAS AROUND TO WITNESS WHAT WAS TAKING PLACE. AS SHE WAS BUSY DOING HER BIG WAIL OUT, SHE FELT SOMETHING TOUCHING HER SOFTLY ON HER HAND. WHEN SHE LOOKED UP, SURPRISED, ALL SHE SAW WAS A LITTLE MAN, AN ELF IMP. HE ASKED HER WHAT THE BIG CRY WAS ALL ABOUT. SHE THEN TOLD HIM EVERYTHING, UNTIL NO MORE EXPLANATIONS WERE LEFT INSIDE HER HEAD. THEN THE IMP TOLD HER HE COULD HELP HER OUT, IF SHE WOULD JUST GIVE HIM SOME OF THE BERRIES THAT SHE HAD JUST GOTTEN FOR HER DESSERTS, WHICH SHE ALSO HAD PLANS FOR. THE WOMAN THEN GAVE THE LITTLE IMP SOME OF THE FRESH BERRIES THAT SHE HAD PICKED. IN RETURN, THE IMP GAVE HER SOMETHING WHITE IN COLOR AND SMALL IN SIZE, AND TOLD HER TO SWALLOW

THAT SOMETHING THAT HE HAD JUST GIVEN TO HER. SHE DID SO, AND THEY TOLD EACH OTHER THEIR GOODBYES AND ALL THE OTHER GOOD STUFF. THEY WENT WHEREVER WAS DESTINED FOR THE TWO OF THEM. YES, SHE DID CONCEIVE SOME BABY SOULS LATER ON IN HER LIFETIME, AND WAS THEN A MUCH HAPPIER SOUL, THANKS TO THAT IMP, WHO JUST HAPPENED TO BE AT THE RIGHT PLACE AT THE RIGHT TIME TO HELP OUT THIS POOR SOUL. SHE WANTED HER VERY OWN CHILDREN TO DO SOME CHORES FOR HER AND HER HUSBAND WHEN THEY GOT TOO OLD TO DO THOSE THINGS FOR THEMSELVES.

EVIL HAND

THIS SMALL AND YOUNG POOR SOUL WENT
OUTDOORS ONE DAY TO PLAY SOME GAMES
WITH HIS FRIENDS, WHO WERE ALREADY OUT
DOING SOME HEAVY GAME ACTIVITIES BEFORE
HIS ARRIVAL TO JOIN IN THEIR FUN FOR THE
DAY, THINGS THAT THEY WERE ENJOYING
IMMENSELY, AND WITH GREAT GUSTO. WHAT
THIS SMALL SOUL DID NOT KNOW WAS THAT
HE WAS ABOUT TO BE ALMOST CAPTURED
AND TAKEN BY SOMETHING, WHICH HE OR
ANY ONE LIVING SOUL WAS ABOUT TO KNOW
THE MEANING OF, AND REASONS FOR, BUT
WOULD HAVE BEEN A VERY BAD ENDING FOR
THE BOY SOUL IN QUESTION. HE WAS OUT
DOING HIS THING OF ENJOYING THE GAMES
AND FUN THAT COMES ALONG WITH SO DOING,
FOR THE BETTER PART OF THE MORNING. AT
ABOUT NOON, HIS SMALL TUMMY TOLD HIM
THAT YES, IT WAS ABOUT THAT TIME AGAIN,
TO HEAD HOME AND HAVE HIS LUNCH BREAK
FROM ALL OF THIS FUN THAT WAS TAKING
PLACE AT THAT VERY MOMENT. KNOWING
THAT HIS MOMMY WOULD HAVE COOKED UP
SOME TASTY BIRD OR FISH SOUP FOR HIM AND
HIS IMMEDIATE FAMILY MEMBERS TO ENJOY,
HE WENT BACK TO HIS HOUSE. WHEN HE GOT

TO HIS HOUSE'S PORCH, HE PROCEEDED TO GO INSIDE HIS HOME THROUGH THE DOOR, BUT WHEN HE WAS ABOUT TO GO INSIDE, SOMETHING GRABBED HIS LEG. BUT HE HELD ON TO THE DOORKNOB, ALL THE WHILE PULLING HIS LEG WITH ALL HIS MIGHT. BUT AFTER SEEING WHAT HAD GOT A HOLD OF HIM, HE WAS PRETTY MUCH SHAKEN UP AND IN SHOCK. HIS MOUTH DRIED UP AND HE COULD NOT EVEN YELL OR SCREAM, AFTER SEEING THAT IT WAS AN EVIL DEMON'S CLAW HAND, ROTTEN AND HAIRY, ALSO SMELLING REALLY BAD. THE EVIL DEMON'S HAND STOPPED HIM COLD IN HIS TRACKS, AND FOR REASONS NOT KNOWN TO THE KID SOUL BOY, THE EVIL DEMON'S HAND WAS NOT ABOUT TO LET GO, BUT TO PULL HIM OUT AND STEAL HIS SOUL FOR SATAN, HIS EVIL KING, WHO ONLY DESTROYS AND KILLS. THE SMALL BOY STARTED TO PANIC, AND WHO WOULDN'T, IF ONE WERE GRABBED FROM BEHIND BY SOMETHING SO EVIL-LOOKING? THIS POOR SMALL SOUL WAS FAST LOSING HIS BATTLE AGAINST THAT SHARP-CLAWED HAND, AND THE INSIDE DOOR WAS STARTING TO CLOSE REALLY SLOWLY. THAT WAS WHEN HIS MOM SHOUTED AT THE TOP OF HER LUNGS, ASKING WHAT WAS THE MATTER, SINCE SHE HAD CLEARLY SEEN HER SON WITH HER VERY OWN EYES ABOUT TO COME IN FOR HIS NOON MEAL, BUT HE WAS RATHER SLOWLY GOING BACK OUT AGAIN, AND THE DOOR WAS CLOSING UP EVER SO

SLOWLY. THE MOM'S YELL SAVED THIS POOR YOUNG SOUL FROM THAT EVIL CLAWED HAND. THE DEVIL'S EVIL DEMON WAS CONTROLLED FROM HARMING THE SMALL SOUL. THAT BOY WAS VERY SCARED AND IN SHOCK BECAUSE OF THAT EVIL THING OUT TO DO HIM GREAT HARM.

BACKWARD SLEDDER

THERE WAS A COMMUNITY POTLATCH SCHEDULED IN ANOTHER SMALL VILLAGE, AND RESIDENTS OF THIS SMALL VILLAGE IN QUESTION HAD BEEN INVITED TO ATTEND ALL THE DANCING AND FOOD PARTIES THAT WERE TO TAKE PLACE DURING THE COURSE OF THE POTLATCH, WHICH WOULD LAST FOR A WEEK OR SO, OR UNTIL EVERYONE WAS HAPPY AND ALL SATISFIED. SO THIS ONE MAN DECIDED FOR HIMSELF THAT HE WOULD ATTEND THAT NEARBY VILLAGE'S PARTY. HE HAD HIS WIFE PREPARE SOME FOOD FOR HIM TO CONSUME DURING THAT DOGSLED RIDE OUT TO THAT OTHER SMALL VILLAGE. HE NEXT WENT OUT TO GET HIS DOG TEAM READY FOR THE TRIP, HITCHING THEM UP TO HIS SLED. AND SO, AFTER ALL WAS SAID AND DONE, HE WENT TO RETRIEVE THE FOOD THAT HIS WIFE HAD PREPARED FOR HIM FOR THIS TRIP, ON WHICH HE, THE MAN SOUL, HOPED THAT ALL WOULD GO WELL FOR HIM. BUT THAT WOULD NOT BE SO FOR THIS SLEDDING MAN. HE ASKED HER FIRST IF SHE WANTED TO ACCOMPANY HIM ON HIS TRAVEL TO THAT OTHER VILLAGE, BUT SHE WISHED HIM A GOOD TRIP AND TOLD HIM TO BE CAREFUL, BUT REFUSED TO COME

ALONG WITH HIM. SO HE TOOK OFF WITHOUT HER. ALL WAS GOING WELL SO FAR FOR THIS SOUL SLEDDER, UNTIL HE HAPPENED TO LOOK BACK AND SAW WHAT SEEMED LIKE ANOTHER DOGTEAM CLOSING IN ON HIM QUICKLY. HE GAVE IT NO MORE THOUGHT. WHEN HE SAW THE OTHER SLEDDER GOING PAST HIM, IT WAS AN UGLY DEMON WITH BIG, EVIL-LOOKING DOGS GOING BACKWARDS. THAT MADE THIS SLED SOUL TURN AROUND AND HEAD ON BACK TO WHERE HE HAD STARTED FROM IN THE FIRST PLACE. HE WAS HOME SO QUICKLY THAT HE HAD NOT EVEN HAD A CHANCE TO REACH THAT OTHER VILLAGE WITH ITS PARTY FESTIVITIES TAKING PLACE AT ABOUT THAT MOMENT. HIS WIFE ASKED HIM WHY IN THE WORLD HE WAS BACK HOME SO QUICKLY. THEN SHE UNDERSTOOD, WHEN HE TOLD HER ALL OF WHAT HAD JUST TAKEN PLACE ALONG THE TRAIL, AND TOLD HER THAT WITHOUT MUCH OF A DOUBT, THAT BACKWARD-SLEDDING DEMON WAS PUSHING AHEAD OF HIM SO THAT HE WOULD HAVE A LITTLE ACCIDENT WITH VERY FATAL CONSEQUENCES FOR HIM AND HIS DOGTEAM. YES, THIS MAN SOUL DID MAKE THAT SLED TRIP TO THAT OTHER VILLAGE THE FOLLOWING DAY. THIS TIME AROUND, HE ASKED SOME OF THE OTHER VILLAGE SOULS TO COME ALONG WITH THEIR DOG TEAMS WITH HIM TO ENJOY THAT POTLATCH TAKING PLACE IN THAT OTHER VILLAGE.

CLOSE CALL WITH DEMONS

THIS BAD MAN SOUL HAD SOMETHING GOING ON IN HIS DAILY GIFE OF LIFE, AND THAT SOMETHING WAS MAKING SURE THAT THOSE IN HIS PRESENCE WOULD FEEL BAD AND WORTHLESS WHENEVER HE WAS PRESENT. ALL THIS BAD STUFF THAT THE BAD MAN WAS DISHING OUT, CONTAMINATING HIS SURROUNDING AREA, WAS ALL DUE TO HIS CHILDHOOD UPBRINGING AND HIS MAD-DOG-TYPE DAD, WHO WAS ALSO PARTIALLY TO BLAME OR COUNTED FOR HIS CURRENT CONDITION, FOR HE HAD HAD A MUCH LESS THAN PERFECT CHILDHOOD. WELL THEN, THE FUTURE WOULD SUDDENLY CHANGE FOR A BETTER PERSON AFTER THE DEVIL'S VERY OWN EVILS WOULD COME AND STAY WITH HIM DAILY. AS WE HAVE SAID BEFORE, DURING THE CLOSING TIME OF HIS BAD PERSON DAYS, HE STARTED HAVING DEMONS PAY HIM A VISIT. THAT, NO DOUBT, WAS TO GO INTO HIS SOUL AND POSSESS HIS MIND AND SOUL. THESE DEMON'S THAT HAD BIG FANGS WITH A BAD ODOR COMING FROM THEIR HAIRY BODIES WOULD OFTEN COME AND ASK HIM, THE BAD SOUL, IF THEY COULD ONLY COME INTO HIM. ALSO, THEY PROMISED HIM THAT THEY

WOULD NOT HURT HIM ONE BIT, AS SOON AS HE ALLOWED THEM TO TAKE POSSESSION OF HIS SOUL, BUT RATHER, TOLD HIM HE WOULD HAVE GREAT STRENGTH AND THAT HE WOULD LIVE FOR A LONG TIME. ALSO, THEY TOLD HIM THAT THEY WOULD BE VERY WILLING TO LEAVE HIS BODY IF HE TOLD THEM TO DO SO, BUT TOLD HIM THEY NEEDED HIS PERMISSION AND GO AHEAD BEFORE THEY ENTERED HIM. THIS WENT ON FOR A WEEK OR SO, WITH THOSE EVIL DEMONS ASKING AROUND. THEN ONE DAY, ONE OF THEM HAPPENED TO TOUCH THIS BAD SOUL'S HAND, AND BOY, IT HAD A BURNING SENSATION WHEN HE WAS TOUCHED. SOON, THE AREA THAT HAD BEEN TOUCHED BECAME GREEN AND STANK. THIS REALLY SCARED THE POOR BAD SOUL, AND SO, HE SOUGHT HELP FROM THE CLERGY TO DRIVE THOSE EVIL, FOUL-SMELLING DEMONS AWAY. AND GUESS WHAT? THE MAN SOON LOST ALL HIS HAIR AND HIS SKIN PEELED OFF. LATER ON, WHEN ALL WAS WELL AGAIN, HIS HAIR GREW AGAIN AND NEW SKIN REPLACED THE OLD SKIN THAT WAS LOST. THE ENDING PART ALSO TURNED OUT GOOD FOR ALL SOULS, BECAUSE THIS BAD SOUL STARTED BEING GOOD TO EVERYONE, AND AFTERWARD, ALL OF THEM STARTED THINKING THAT YES, THEY DO FIT IN, AND YES, THEY ARE WORTH IT ALL. THE LITTLE KIDS ESPECIALLY WERE NOW HELPED OUT BY THIS NOW GOOD SOUL, FORMERLY A BAD, BAD SOUL.

BATHROOM CLOSE CALL

THIS MAN HAD AN EXPERIENCE THAT HE WOULD NOT EASILY FORGET FOR HIS ENTIRE GIFT OF DAILY LIVING. WHAT HAPPENED THAT FATEFUL DAY? HE HAD A CALL TO PUT HIS TOILET TO GOOD USE, AND HE DID JUST THAT. HE MADE HIS TRIP OFTEN, BUT THIS TIME, THERE WAS A DEMON. YES, ONE OF THOSE THAT MAKES SURE THAT EVERYONE, ESPECIALLY ALL LIVING SOULS CARRYING ON THEIR ONLY GIFTS OF DAILY LIFE, WOULD LIVE MISERY-FILLED LIVES. HOW DO THEY, THE EVIL DEMONS, DO IT? WELL, THE TRUTH TO BE KNOWN TO ALL LIVING SOULS IS THIS: THEY GET ORDERED TO DO SO FROM THE CHIEF EVIL ONE HIMSELF, TO WHISPER INTO THE EARS OF EVERY LIVING SOUL, TO DO EVIL ON ONE ANOTHER AND OTHER STUFF, TO LEAD AS MANY SOULS AS THEY CAN INTO EVERLASTING PUNISHMENT BY A VERY, VERY HOT FIRE, WHERE THERE WILL BE NO REST, NO FOOD, NO SLEEP, AND NO WATER. TO MAKE A LONG STORY SHORT, THERE WILL BE A VERY HIGH DEGREE OF CONSTANT SUFFERING AND CRYING. WELL THEN, HE WAS NOT HAVING TOO MANY THOUGHTS, WHEN HE THOUGHT THAT HE HAD HEARD A VERY FAINT KNOCK ON THE

TOILET DOOR. HE PLAYED ALONG, WHICH WAS HIS BAD MISTAKE. FOR AS SOON AS HE HAD SAID COME IN, A VERY WEIRD THING HAPPENED AND WHAT HE SAW FREAKED HIM OUT REALLY BADLY. FIRST, ITS HAIRY LEGS APPEARED, THEN THE BODY CAME IN FROM UNDERNEATH THE DOORWAY SPACE. IT WAS A BIG HAIRY SPIDER COMING IN BACKWARDS AND COMING TOWARDS HIM, STOPPING ONCE IN A WHILE, AS IF SMELLING THE AIR. THIS POOR SOUL COULD NOT EVEN MOVE A MUSCLE, BUT WAS SUDDENLY FROZEN ON HIS TOILET SEAT. ALL THE WHILE, THAT DEMON IN A SPIDER'S FORM WAS COMING CLOSER AND CLOSER, UNTIL IT WAS NEAR HIS FOOT. THAT WAS WHEN THIS UNMOVING SOUL THOUGHT OF STEPPING ON IT. AS SOON AS HE STEPPED ON THAT BACKWARD-MOVING SPIDER, HE HEARD A VERY LOUD, EVIL SCREAM. SUDDENLY, HIS MOVEMENTS WERE ABLE TO FUNCTION, AND A FOUL-SMELLING FOG SUDDENLY WAS COVERING HIS WHOLE LATRINE. LATER, AFTER GETTING HIS HEAD STRAIGHTENED OUT, HE FOUND OUT THAT THERE WAS A SMALL HOLE IN HIS BATHROOM FLOOR GOING ALL THE WAY THROUGH. AFTERWARDS, THIS MAN SOUL IN QUESTION ALWAYS HAD A FUNNY FEELING WHENEVER THE NATURE CALL CAME FOR HIM TO USE HIS TOILET AND ALL. BUT ALL IN ALL, HIS ONLY THOUGHTS WERE FOCUSED ON THE THOUGHT THAT ALL'S WELL THAT ENDS WELL, FOR ALL GOOD SOULS AND BAD SOULS ALIKE.

SHAKING TENT

THESE THREE MAN SOULS, ONE FINE SUNNY, CALM DAY, HAD THEIR LITTLE GET TOGETHER, AND THEREFORE MADE THEIR MINDS UP AND ALL AGREED THAT THEY WOULD GO CAMPING OUT AT A SMALL CREEK NOT TOO FAR FROM THEIR BIRTHPLACE--IN THAT CASE, THEIR HOME VILLAGE. AFTER GETTING ALL THEIR GEAR FOR THEIR TRIP READY, THEY THEN WENT OUT WITH ONE OF THE SOULS' BOATS. THEIR TRIP TO THEIR DESTINATION, WHICH THEY KNEW WOULD NOT TAKE TOO LONG TO REACH, AWAITED THEM WITH OPEN ARMS, SO THEY THOUGHT. AFTER REACHING THAT PLACE, THEY CHOSE A SMALL GRASSY AREA ON WHICH THEY PLANNED TO SPEND THE NIGHT. AFTER THEY HAD SET UP THEIR TENT, THEY THEN PROCEDED TO UNLOAD ALL THEIR FOOD ITEMS AND THEIR SLEEPING GEAR INTO THE TENT THAT THEY HAD JUST SET UP. AFTER ALL WAS SAID AND DONE, THE THREE VERY ALIVE LIVING SOULS THEN WENT OUT TO HUNT SOME BIRDS THAT WERE IN THAT AREA. TOWARDS THE EVENING HOURS, AFTER RETURNING BACK TO THEIR CAMPSITE, ONE OF THE HUNTING SOULS PLUCKED AND COOKED UP A RATHER FAT

GOOSE THAT HAD BEEN GOT OR HAD BEEN SHOT DOWN BY ONE OF THE HUNTER SOULS. AFTER A HARDY AND TASTY MEAL, THEY GOT READY TO SLEEP IT OFF. SO THEY WERE LYING AROUND, TRYING TO GET SOME SHUT-EYE AFTER THAT FOOD HAD BEEN EATEN UP. AS THEY WERE ABOUT TO LOSE IT ALL TO LA-LA-LAND, SOMETHING QUITE STRANGE THEN HAPPENED. WHAT TOOK PLACE WAS THIS: THOUGH THE NIGHT WAS VERY CALM AND NO WIND WAS ACTIVE, LO AND BEHOLD, THEY HEARD A FAINT SOUND, GETTING LOUDER ALL THE TIME. AFTER IT HAD GOTTEN QUITE LOUD, THEIR TENT STARTED DANCING AND SHAKING QUITE WILDLY. THIS EPISODE MADE THESE SOULS QUITE SCARED, SINCE THEY KNEW IT WAS A VERY CALM NIGHT. AFTER GETTING IT ALL FIGURED OUT, THEY DECIDED FOR THEMSELVES THAT THEY WOULD MOVE OUT TO A MUCH SAFER PLACE. THIS THEY DID VERY GLADLY, AND WITH ONLY ONE THING ON THEIR MINDS: WOULD THEIR TENT START ITS WILD DANCING AND GET ALL SHAKEN UP AGAIN? MUCH TO THEIR SURPRISE, THIS DID NOT HAPPEN, BUT RATHER, THINGS WENT QUITE SMOOTHLY FOR THESE THREE HUNTING SOULS. THAT WAS AFTER MOVING TO A MUCH DIFFERENT, AND ALSO SAFER, SPOT. THERE THEY AGAIN SET UP THEIR TENT. AFTER MUCH SWEATY, BACK-BREAKING WORK, ALL WAS READY AGAIN FOR THEM TO SPEND THEIR NIGHT IN THAT MUCH SAFER SPOT.

THE FOLLOWING DAY, THEY TRAVELED BACK TO THEIR VILLAGE WITHOUT SO MUCH AS A SINGLE BIRD BEING SHOT DOWN BY THESE HUNTING LIVING SOULS, SINCE THEY WERE QUITE SHAKEN UP AND A LITTLE SCARED OF WHAT HAD TAKEN PLACE THE PRECEDING DAY. AND THAT WAS THAT THE TENT THEY HAD TRUSTED IN HAD DONE ITS PART OF SCARING THEM QUITE A BIT.

DEAD BABY GHOST

THESE TWO VERY LOVING PARENTS ONCE WERE OUT IN THEIR FISH CAMP WITH THEIR SMALL CHILD, FOR WHOM THEY JUST WERE IN FULL ADORATION, AND ALSO LOVED VERY MUCH. SO ALL WAS GOING WELL FOR THESE SOULS WHO LOVED EACH OTHER. BUT ONE DAY, THEIR ONLY SMALL CHILD CAME DOWN WITH A VERY HIGH FEVER AND WAS VERY SICK. WHAT THE LOVING PARENTS TRIED TO DO WAS TO NURSE THEIR VERY MUCH LOVED SMALL CHILD BACK INTO GOOD HEALTH. THEY DID GIVE HIM SOME TRADITIONAL MEDICATIONS, HOPING THAT MAY MAKE HIM WELL AGAIN. BUT FOR SOME REASON OR REASONS THAT WERE NOT KNOWN TO THEM, THE TRADITIONAL MEDICATION WAS NOT ABLE TO MAKE THEIR SMALL BABY WELL, MUCH TO THEIR DISMAY AND DISAPPOINTMENT. THEY WORKED HARD TAKING TURNS, BOTH DAY AND NIGHT, BUT DESPITE THEIR ONGOING AND TIRELESS EFFORTS, THE SMALL SOUL WAS TAKEN AWAY FROM THEM, IN A FORM OF BODILY DEATH. THIS, OF COURSE, DEEPLY HURT THEM, AND ALSO, THEIR HEARTS WERE BROKEN AND THEY WERE VERY MUCH EMOTIONALLY PAINED. AND SO, THAT BEING

SAID AND DONE WITH, THEY PREPARED THE SMALL SOUL'S BODY FOR BURIAL, NOT TOO FAR FROM THEIR CAMPSITE, AND PLACED HIM BENEATH THE HEARTLESS GROUND. BUT DUE TO THEIR PAST LOVE FOR THAT SMALL SOUL, THEY PLAYED THAT HE WAS STILL ALIVE AND WELL. THE MOTHER MADE HIM BABY CLOTHES AND WHENEVER SHE COOKED, BROUGHT SOME COOKED FOOD TO HIS BURIAL SITE. DOING SUCH WAS VERY WRONG, INDEED. FOR ABOUT A WEEK OR SO, THEY ACTED AS IF THE SOUL CHILD WAS STILL ALIVE, AND THE MOTHER KEPT BRINGING HIM FOOD. SOON THEREAFTER, THE FOOD BEING BROUGHT AND THE CLOTHES OFFERED STARTED TURNING UP MISSING, OR GONE FROM THE PLACEMENT AREA WHERE IT HAD BEEN BROUGHT TO. AND THE OTHER SCARY PART WAS THAT THE CRYING OF A BABY COULD SOON BE HEARD FROM THE BURIAL SITE AREA, AS IF IT NEEDED TO BE COMFORTED. WHEN ALL THESE UNUSUAL OCCURRENCES STARTED TO TAKE PLACE, THE LOVING SOULS DECIDED TO MOVE BACK TO THEIR VILLAGE BECAUSE ALL THESE UNUSUAL THINGS THAT WERE GOING ON WERE VERY MUCH OUT OF PLACE. AND ALSO, THEY WERE GETTING QUITE SCARED OF ALL THAT WAS TAKING PLACE IN THEIR IMMEDIATE CAMPING AREA. SO THEY PACKED WHAT LITTLE THEY OWNED AND MOVED BACK TO THEIR HOME VILLAGE, AND AFTERWARDS, THEY CHOSE ANOTHER CAMPSITE WHENEVER

THEY WENT OUT TO HUNT OR GATHER SOME EDIBLE PLANTS AND/OR ROOTS. THIS BABY GHOST HAUNTING WAS A PROBLEM THAT THEY, THE LOVING SOULS, HAD BROUGHT AGAINST THEMSELVES, AND WAS A VERY VALUABLE LESSON THAT WHENEVER ONE DIES, THE VERY ALIVE SOUL GOES EITHER TO A GOOD PLACE OF HAPPINESS, OR IS TAKEN BY DEMONS BELOW THE EARTH, TO BE TORTURED BY FIRE, BY THE VERY EVIL DEMONS, AS ORDERED BY THEIR MASTER, THE MOST EVIL ONE HIMSELF, SATAN.

DEMON-CONTROLLED PARENTS

THESE TWO VERY EVIL-MINDED SOULS HAD A FIRST BORN CHILD, WHICH WAS A SMALL GIRL. AND FOR SOME REASON, KNOWN ONLY TO THEIR EVIL NATURES, THEY DID NOT WANT THAT CHILD. WHEN NO ONE WANTED TO ADOPT THAT YOUNG POOR SOUL, THEY MADE UP THEIR MINDS THAT THEY WOULD SEND HER OFF TO AN EARLY GRAVE. AND WHAT THEY TRIED TO DO WAS VERY EVIL IN THE EYES OF THEIR FELLOW VILLAGERS, AND ALSO IN OTHER VILLAGES, DUE TO THE FACT THAT THE EVIL THING THAT THEY WERE DOING, ACCORDING TO THEIR WISHES, WAS CIRCULATING AS BIG NEWS AMONG THE OTHER SOULS, LIVING AND KNOWING WHAT WAS GOING ON. FOR THESE TWO EVIL-HEARTED SOULS WERE DOING WHAT THEY WERE DOING VERY OPENLY, AND WERE NOT ABOUT TO START LOVING THAT SMALL POOR CHILD SOUL ANYTIME SOON. WELL THEN, WHAT WERE MR. AND MRS. EVIL-MINDED BAD LIVING SOULS DOING? WHAT THEY WERE DOING WAS THIS VERY EVIL TRUTH. THEY KEPT THAT SMALL POOR SOUL UNDERNEATH THEIR BED, INSIDE A GALVANIZED STEEL WASHTUB, AND KEPT HER THERE INSIDE THAT STEEL TUB DAY IN

AND DAY OUT, NEVER LETTING HER OUT. AND LITTLE FOOD AND WATER WAS GIVEN TO HER--NOT MUCH, BUT IT KEPT HER ALIVE. AND THE OTHER SAD THING WAS THAT THEY MADE HER SLEEP INSIDE THE STEEL TUB WITHOUT ANY BLANKET, DESPITE THE COLD WINTER WEATHER. BUT THAT POOR CHILD DID NOT FREEZE TO DEATH, NOR DID SHE DIE FROM THIRST, OR STARVE TO DEATH. IT WAS AS IF SOMETHING UNSEEN WAS LOOKING AFTER HER DURING THE COLD WINTER NIGHTS. AND WHENEVER ANYONE VISITED THE DEMON-CONTROLLED MOM AND DAD, THEY WOULD SEE THAT SMALL CHILD SOUL, PEERING WITH BIG, SAD EYES FROM HER WASHING TUB HOLDING PLACE BENEATH THE BAD SOULS' BED. SHE SOON GREW UP, FOR SHE WAS IN THAT TUB BENEATH THE BED FOR OVER SEVEN YEARS. WHEN SHE WAS EIGHT, THE VERY EVIL PARENTS GAVE HER AWAY TO A VERY LOVING FAMILY IN ANOTHER VILLAGE. BUT DESPITE THIS LOVING FAMILY'S EFFORTS TO MAKE HER FEEL WELCOME, SHE WOULD NOT LET THEM TOUCH HER, NOR CUDDLE HER. AND WHENEVER THEY GAVE THE SMALL POOR SOUL A BOWL OF FOOD, SHE WOULD START SNARLING AT ALL THE OTHERS, HOLDING HER BOWL OF FOOD. SHE WAS ALSO VERY MEAN-TEMPERED, AND WOULD OFTEN SCRATCH AND CLAW THE PEOPLE WHO WERE TRYING THEIR BEST TO COMFORT HER. AND SHE WOULD START CRYING AND SCREAMING

REALLY LOUDLY. DUE TO HER VERY BAD UPBRINGING, THIS POOR SMALL CHILD SOON GOT SICK AND WOULD NOT GET WELL. SOON SHE HAPPENED TO DIE FROM HER SICKNESS, JUST WHEN SHE WAS ABOUT TO START LIVING WITH A VERY LOVING FAMILY, AND THE ADOPTIVE MOM DREAMED THAT A VERY NICE-LOOKING ANGEL CAME DOWN FROM HEAVEN AND TOOK HER SOUL UP, AFTER WHICH THE DREAMER IN QUESTION SEEMED TO BE AT A VERY HAPPY STAGE.

MARRIED DOG

THERE WAS YOUNG WOMAN WHOM MEN OF THIS CERTAIN VILLAGE LIKED VERY MUCH, FOR SHE WAS CUTE AND ALL THE OTHER GOOD FACIAL FEATURES SHOWED ON HER FACE. THE THING WAS THAT SHE KEPT REFUSING ALL HER SUITERS; FOR MARRIAGE PURPOSES, THE ANSWER WAS THE SAME OLD STORY, AND THAT WAS THAT HER ANSWER WOULD BE NO, TO ALL THE YOUNG MAN SOULS THAT WERE LIVING IN THE VERY SAME VILLAGE AS HERS AND TELLING HER THAT THEY WOULD TAKE GOOD CARE OF HER. HER MOM WOULD OFTEN ASK HER WHY SHE WOULD NOT GIVE HERSELF AWAY AND GET HITCHED TO A YOUNG MAN SOUL, AND HER ANSWER WOULD BE THAT SHE WAS NOT READY TO BE ON HER OWN. THIS WENT ON FOR A COUPLE OF YEARS, UNTIL SHE WAS IN HER LATE TEENS. FINALLY, ONE DAY, HER MOM BROKE APART AND SHOUTED AT HER, "WHY DO YOU KEEP REFUSING TO LET THESE YOUNG SOULS BE YOUR HUSBAND? DO YOU WANT A DOG FOR A HUSBAND?" THE YOUNG GIRL SOUL'S MOM WAS VERY SURPRISED AND SHOCKED WHEN SHE SAID THAT YES, SHE WAS VERY WILLING TO GET MARRIED TO THIS CERTAIN BIG ANIMAL

DOG. SO SHE DID GET TOGETHER WITH THAT BIG DOG, AND THEN SHE AND HER DOG HUSBAND MOVED OUT TO THE WILDERNESS TO SAVE FACE. VERY SOON, THESE TWO HAD CHILDREN WHO WERE ONE HALF HUMAN AND THE OTHER HALF DOG. THEIR CHILDREN, WHO WERE HALF-ANIMAL, SOON SAW THAT THEY WOULD HAVE PROBLEMS WITH THE OTHER REGULAR LIVING SOULS, AND THAT THEY WOULD NOT BE ACCEPTABLE, NO MATTER WHAT OR WHEREVER THEY WENT. ONE DAY IN THEIR TEENS, THEY MADE PLANS THAT THEY WOULD TAKE CARE OF THEIR LITTLE PROBLEM. THEIR PLAN WAS TO KILL THEIR DOG DAD, AND THEN KILL EACH OTHER OFF. THEY ALL AGREED TO THEIR PLAN TO GET RID OF THEIR DAD, AND AFTERWARDS, WHEN THE DOG DAD WENT TO HUNT FOOD FOR THEM, THEY MADE THEIR PREPARATIONS TO KILL HIM. AS SOON AS HE GOT BACK FROM HIS FOOD-GATHERING DUTIES, THEY SAW THEIR DOG DAD AND THEY WERE READY TO GET RID OF HIM. AS SOON AS HE CAME HOME WITH SOME FOOD THAT HE HAD CAUGHT, THEY SPRANG INTO ACTION AND ACTED AS IF THEY WERE VERY GLAD TO SEE HIM COME BACK WITH FOOD FOR THEM AND THEIR REGULAR MOM. BUT AS SOON AS HE LET HIS GUARD DOWN, THEY, THE HALF-DOG AND HALF-HUMANS, MAULED HIM AND TORE HIM UP REALLY WELL UNTIL HE WAS NO LONGER AMONG THE LIVING. THEN, AFTER ALL WAS SAID AND DONE, THEY STABBED

EACH OTHER UNTIL THEY WERE ALL DEAD. THEIR MOM WAS GREATLY PAINED BY THEIR ACTIONS, BUT GOT OVER IT SOON, AND WENT HOME, WHERE THIS TIME AROUND, SHE GOT MARRIED TO A REAL HUMAN AND NOT JUST ANY OLD DOG.

DEMON-CONTROLLED CLAW

THIS VERY YOUNG SOUL GIRL, WHO LIVED IN THIS SMALL VILLAGE, WOULD, ONE FATEFUL EVENING, BE A TRUE BELIVER OF WHAT CAME OUT FROM THE WISDOM OF HER ELDERS' SAYINGS. FOR SHE HAD SOME DOUBTS AND QUESTIONS ON HER MIND THAT SHE ALONE CONTROLLED. WHAT THE ELDERS CAUTIONED HER AND ALL THE OTHER YOUNG SOULS OF HER SAME VILLAGE ABOUT WAS THIS: IF IT IS DARK OUTSIDE, DO NOT, UNDER ANY CIRCUMSTANCES, GO OUT WITH PIECES OF FISHSKIN INSIDE YOUR MOUTHS. BE SURE TO EAT EVERYTHING UP BEFORE LEAVING ANY HOUSE IN WHICH YOU HAVE BEEN EATING. SHE AND ALL THE OTHER YOUNG SOULS WOULD OFTEN HEAR THIS BEING TOLD BY ALL THE OLD LIVING SOULS, WHO WERE TELLING THEM THE RIGHT WAY OF LIVING ONE'S LIFE. WHENEVER THEY HAPPENED TO BE GUIDING HANDS AT WORK, LETTING THE YOUNG SOULS KNOW WHAT LIES AHEAD IN THEIR FUTURE YEARS YET TO COME, THEY CAUTIONED THEM THAT AN EVIL DEMON-CONTROLLED, CLAWED HAND WOULD SUDDENLY APPEAR FROM NOWHERE AND COVER UP THEIR MOUTHS. ALSO, THE NOSE WOULD BE INCLUDED IN COVERING

EVERYTHING UP. THIS WOULD, OF COUSE, MAKE THE SOUL IN QUESTION NOT BE ABLE TO BREATHE AT ALL. SINCE THIS SOMEWHAT YOUNG GIRL SOUL WAS NOT THE TYPE THAT CAN BE SCARED EASILY, AND ALSO HAD DOUBTS OF ANY CLAWS HANGING OUT IN THE PORCH OF HOUSES, SHE DECIDED TO TEST THIS SAYING THAT, FOR HER, SEEMED LIKE JUST A STORY THAT HAD BEEN MADE UP, AND ALSO HAD NOT A SINGLE TRUTH IN IT. AND SHE DID MAKE HER TERRIBLE MISTAKE WITH DEMON-CONTROLLED CLAWS, WHICH, YES, DID AS THE VILLAGE ELDERS HAD OFTEN TOLD HER AND THE OTHER YOUNGSTERS IN HER VILLAGE. ONE EVENING, THIS UNBELIEVING YOUNG SOULFUL GIRL WENT OUT OF HER FRIEND'S HOUSE, ALL THE WHILE CHEWING ON A PIECE OF FISHSKIN THAT THE MOM OF HER FRIEND HAD GIVEN HER, TO CONSUME AND ENJOY THE TASTE OF THAT FISHSKIN. WELL THEN, AS SHE WAS GOING OUT, HEADING TO HER PLACE, THERE WAS A VERY DARK PORCH THAT SHE HAD TO GO THROUGH FIRST. WELL, AS SOON AS SHE WAS INSIDE THE PORCH AREA, AN EVIL, FOUL-ODORED HAND, FULL OF HAIR AND BIG-CLAWED, GOT A HOLD OF HER BREATHING AREA AND HELD ON. THE POOR GIRL SOUL THEN FOUND OUT THAT SHE COULD NOT BREATHE IN AND OUT. PRETTY SOON, SHE STARTED TO PANIC FROM HER CURRENT SITUATION WITH THAT CLAW STILL HANGING ON LIKE THERE WAS NO

TOMORROW. SHE WAS GETTING QUITE BLUE IN HER FACE AND THE GAS PRESSURE INSIDE HER STOMACH WAS QUICKLY BUILDING UP. AFTER MUCH STRUGGLING AND FIGHTING, TRYING HER BEST TO DECLAW HER MOUTH AREA, SHE LET OUT GAS LOUDLY, FROM OUT OF THE BLUE, DUE TO THE FACT THAT SHE, THE GAS-RELEASING YOUNG GIRL SOUL, WAS VERY WEAK FROM BEING AIRLESS AND ALSO SCARED STIFF. AS SOON AS THE LOUD GAS WAS RELEASED, THE EVIL DEMON-CONTROLLED, HAIRY, FOUL-ODORED HAND LET GO WITH A POPPING SOUND, AND THE PIECE OF FISHSKIN SHOT OUT OF THIS YOUNG GIRL'S MOUTH, TO THE INSIDE AREA OF THAT PORCH, SOMEWHERE. THEN THIS POOR GIRL RAN HOME AS FAST AS HER LEGS COULD GO, NOW A TRUE BELIEVER THAT WHAT HAD BEEN TOLD BY HER ELDERS WAS INDEED VERY TRUE.

NEVER HIT DEMONS

ONE EVENING, THIS YOUNG MAN WAS MAKING A STEAM BATH, AND HE WAS USING VERY DRY WOOD FOR HIS CURRENT CHORE OF MAKING HIS STEAM, WHICH HE KNEW WOULD BE QUITE HOT, DUE TO THE USE OF VERY DRY DRIFTWOOD. HE CHOPPED UP THE WOOD FOR USE IN HIS UPCOMING STEAM BATH, WHICH HE HIMSELF HAD GATHERED THAT PRECEDING MORNING FROM THE BEACH AREA THAT WAS NOT TOO EXTREMELY FAR FROM THE AREA WEST OF HIS VILLAGE, IN WHICH HE, THE SOUL STEAMING MAN IN QUESTION, WAS BORN, AND NOW EXISTED IN ITS IMMEDIATE AREA. AFTER ALL HAD BEEN SAID AND DONE, HE SOON WAS GOOD AND READY. SO HE FILLED UP HIS FIFTY-FIVE-GALLON WOOD STOVE DRUM WITH THOSE REALLY DRY DRIFTWOOD PIECES THAT HE WAS GLAD ABOUT. HE WAS ALSO HAPPY THAT HE WAS ABOUT TO HAVE HIS RELAX TIME, AND HAVE THE HOT HEAT SOAK UP INTO HIS SOMEWHAT ACHING BODY, WHICH HE KNEW WOULD BE GREATLY RELIEVED AFTER HIS HOT STEAM BATH. HE DID NOT FORGET THAT HIS BODY ACHES WOULD SOMEHOW DISAPPEAR AND BE REPLACED WITH A NEW BODY THAT WAS LIKE NEW,

WITH NO ACHES OR PAIN PRESENT. SOON, HIS STEAM HOUR WAS UNDERWAY, AND HE WAS GREATLY ENJOYING HIS TIME INSIDE HIS VERY WARMED-UP SWEAT HOUSE, TAKING HIS RESTS NOW AND THEN TO COOL OFF HIS VERY MUCH HEATED-UP BODY. AFTER ABOUT HIS THIRD ROUND OF HIS MUCH NEEDED ACTIVITY, WHILE HE WAS INSIDE POURING HOT WATER ONTO THE ROCKS, SO THAT THEY WOULD PRODUCE GREAT HEAT IN STEAM FORM, HE DID HAPPEN TO HEAR A KNOCK ON THE OUTSIDE DOOR OF HIS SAID STEAM HOUSE. THINKING THAT IT WAS ANOTHER SOUL COMING TO JOIN HIM IN HIS HAPPY HOUR, HE SHOUTED AT THE KNOCKER THAT YES, THE PLACE WAS YET HOT AND ENJOYABLE. BUT HE GOT NO RESPONSE, AND NO ONE CAME IN. AFTER SOME TIME HAD PASSED, HE HEARD ANOTHER KNOCK. AFTER SHOUTING AGAIN TO COME RIGHT IN, WHEN NO ONE CAME, HE GOT SOMEWHAT MAD, THINKING THAT SOME CHILDEN SOULS WERE TRYING TO SCARE HIM OR WERE TRYING TO PLAY SOME TRICKS DURING HIS MUCH NEEDED HAPPY HOUR. WHEN NO ONE CAME, HE GOT A HOLD OF HIS WASH BASIN, THINKING TO HIMSELF THAT HE WOULD TEACH THEM A LESSON THAT THEY WOULD NOT BE ABLE TO FORGET ANYTIME SOON. BUT WHEN HE REACHED THE OUTSIDE WORLD, ALL HE SAW WAS AN EVIL, EVIL DEMON WITH GLOWING EVIL EYES STARING AT HIM. HE WAS BOTH SCARED AND WAS ALSO

STILL MAD, SO HE STRUK THE EVIL THING WITH THE BASIN THAT HE WAS HOLDING. AS SOON AS HE HAD DONE SO, HIS MIND BECAME BLANK, AND THE VERY NEXT THING, WHEN HE FINALLY REGAINED HIS SENSES, HE FOUND HIMSELF LYING ON THE GROUND WITH A BIG LUMP ON HIS HEAD AND STILL NAKED. AFTER HIS LITTLE INCIDENT WITH THAT UGLY AND EVIL-ODORED DEMON, HE MADE SURE THAT ONE OF HIS FELLOW SOULS WAS INVITED BY HIM TO ENJOY HIS HAPPY BODY-ACHES-RELIEF SESSIONS WITH HIM, FROM THERE ON AFTER.

BOY SAVED BY LITTLE IMP

A MOTHER AND A SMALL SOULFUL CHILD WERE OUT ONE DAY ON THE RIVER. THESE TWO LIVING SOULS WERE ON FOOD-GATHERING DUTIES BEING CARRIED OUT BY JUST THE TWO OF THEM. THAT IS, THEY HAD BEEN OUT ON THAT RIVER FOR THE BETTER PART OF THE MORNING, SPEARING SOME FRESH FISH, WHICH THEY HAD HAD PRETTY GOOD LUCK WITH, AS FAR AS EVERYTHING GOES, CONCERNING WHAT HAD BEEN SPEARED BY JUST THOSE TWO LIVING SOULS. AT ABOUT THE NOON TIME HOUR, THEY WERE GETTING QUITE FAMISHED, DUE TO HAVE BEEN ACTIVE SINCE THE EARLY MORNING HOURS, AND HAVING CAUGHT SOME NUMBER OF FISH FROM THAT SAID FISH-FILLED RIVER. SO THE MOTHER OF THAT SOMEWHAT YOUNG CHILD TOLD HIM THAT SHE WAS GOING TO COOL SOME LUNCH FOR THE TWO OF THEM AFTER SHE HAD GATHERED SOME DRY TWIGS AND GRASSES FOR THE JOB. WHILE SHE WAS ON HER CHORE OF GETTING THINGS DONE, SHE TOLD HIM, HER YOUNG SON, THAT IS, TO GO AHEAD AND KEEP SPEARING FOR MORE FISH. AND THAT WAS JUST WHAT THE SMALL SOUL DID. AFTER SOME TIME HAD PASSED, SHE

HAD BEEN OUT IN THE WOODS FOR QUITE A SPELL, WHEN SHE HAPPENED TO HEAR HER SMALL SON SHOUTING AND MAKING LOUD NOISES FROM THE DIRECTION OF THE VERY MERCILESS RIVER. SHE DROPPED ALL HER GATHERED TWIGS AND GRASS, AND RAN AS FAST AS HER LEGS COULD CARRY HER TO THE AREA THAT THEY HAD BEEN SPEARING THE FISH FROM, WHICH WAS QUITE DEEP, ABOUT TEN FEET OR SO TO ITS BOTTOM. BUT HER SMALL SON WAS NOWHERE TO BE SEEN, AND HIS SPEAR WAS WASHED AND STUCK ON THE NEARBY RIVER BANK. SHE THEN RAN DOWNRIVER, LOOKING FOR HER SON, HOPING THAT HE WAS STILL ALIVE. MUCH TO HER DISAPPOINTMENT, SHE SAW HIM UNDER THE RIVER ON THE SANDBARED AREA. SHE WALKED ON THE SHALLOW BOTTOM AND RETRIEVED THE BODY OF HER MUCH-LOVED SON, BUT FOUND HIM NOT BREATHING. THAT WAS WHEN SHE REALIZED THAT HE HAD JUST GIVEN UP THE GHOST, AND WAS NOW VERY DEAD. SO SHE STARTED CRYING LOUDLY, FOR SHE LOVED HIM VERY MUCH. AFTER A MINUTE OR SO, SHE HEARD SOMETHING AND HAPPENED TO LOOK UP FROM HER CRYING. SHE SAW AN UGLY LITTLE IMP WITH A SORT OF ROTTED-OUT LOOKING FACE LOOKING AT HER WITH A FUNNY SMILE ON HIS LITTLE FACE. WHAT THE LITTLE IMP TOLD HER WAS THIS: "I CAN BRING YOUR SON BACK TO LIFE, IF ONLY YOU WOULD COOK ME UP SOME OF THOSE FRESH FISH

THAT YOU HAVE JUST SPEARED OUT OF THE RIVER." BELIEVING HIM WITH ALL HER HEART, SHE THEN TOLD HIM THAT YES, SHE WOULD DO AS THE IMP HAD JUST SAID, AND HANDED HIM HER SON, WHOM SHE KNEW WAS VERY DEAD. SHE WENT ABOUT CUTTING UP SOME FISH; WHILE DOING SO, SHE SAW THE IMP LAYING HER SON DOWN AND PRESSING ON HIS STOMACH. SHE SAW WATER COMING OUT THROUGH HIS MOUTH. THE NEXT THING SHE SAW WAS THE IMP, SEEMING TO BREATHE INTO HER YOUNG SON'S MOUTH. A LITTLE WHILE LATER, SHE HEARD HER SON COUGHING, AND THAT GOT HER EXCITED, KNOWING THAT HER SON WOULD LIVE AFTER ALL. AFTER ALL HAD BEEN SAID AND DONE, THEY SAID THEIR THANK YOUS TO EACH OTHER, THE LITTLE UGLY IMP, FULL OF FRESHLY COOKED FISH, AND THE MOM SOUL, WITH A VERY MUCH ALIVE AND WELL SON, WHO WAS BROUGHT BACK AMONG THE LIVING SOULS WITH THE HELP OF THAT LITTLE UGLY MAN.

MAN WANTING TO BE GHOST

THIS ONE LIVING MAN SOUL WAS QUITE OBSESSED WITH THE OTHER SIDE, AFTER ONE'S PASSING OR DEATH, AND HE WOULD OFTEN WONDER WHAT THE OTHER SIDE WAS HIDING FROM ALL LIVING SOULS, WHO WERE VERY MUCH ALIVE, LIVING OUT THEIR GIFTS OF THEIR VERY PRECIOUS LIVES. ON A DAILY BASIS, AFTER SOME PERIOD OF TIME HAD PASSED, THE MAN, WITH HIS VERY BAD INTENTIONS OF LOSING IT ALL TO MECILESS DEATH, WAS THINKING OUT HOW HE COULD END IT ALL, WHICH, HE DID NOT KNOW, HAD ITS VERY BAD SIDES HIDDEN. IT WAS NOT ABOUT TO REVEAL ITSELF TO ANY VERY ALIVE SOULS, OR WHAT SECRETS IT HELD AFTER ONE'S PASSING. THE MAN, WANTING TO MAKE HIS MISTAKE OF ENDING IT ALL, WOULD OFTEN THINK OF HOW HE WOULD END IT ALL. BUT HE WAS ALSO SCARED THAT HE WOULD ONLY END UP AS A CRIPPLED SOUL IF HE WAS NOT SUCCESSFUL WITH HIS PLANS, WHICH HE HAD THOUGHT ABOUT ON A DAILY BASIS. SO ONE FATEFUL DAY, HE HAD A PERFECT PLAN THOUGHT OUT, BY HIMSELF. HE WOULD HIRE AND PAY THIS KNOWN BAD MAN SOUL, WHOM EVERYONE IN HIS HOME VILLAGE KNEW TO BE

A VERY EVIL-MINDED LIVING SOUL, AND WHO WAS SUSPECTED IN A COUPLE OF VERY BAD DEEDS CARRIED OUT BY SOMEONE IN THAT SAID SMALL VILLAGE. SO, HE HAPPENED TO PAY THIS VERY EVIL SOUL WITH FOOD AND SOME HUNTING GEAR, WHICH HE HOPED WOULD PLEASE THE BAD MAN, AND MAKE HIM DO AS HE HAD REQUESTED. THEY MADE PLANS THAT THE MAN SOUL, WHO WANTED TO MAKE HIS MISTAKE OF A LIFETIME, WOULD BE PUBLICLY ACCUSED BY THE EVIL SOUL OF THEIVERY OF HIS EARTHLY POSSESSIONS, AND WOULD BE STABBED TO DEATH AFTER A MUCH PLAYED-OUT, HEATED ARGUMENT BY JUST THE TWO OF THEM. THIS, OF COUSE, PLEASED THE EVIL-MINDED MAN, BECAUSE HIS REPUTATION WOULD BE THAT HE WAS A VERY EVIL-MINDED MAN, INDEED. SO THE FOLLOWING DAY, THEY THEREFORE CARRIED OUT WHAT SEEMED LIKE A VERY REAL THING THAT TOOK PLACE. THEY GOT INTO THEIR VERY WELL PLANNED-OUT ARGUMENT VERY LOUDLY, SO THAT EVERY SOUL WOULD KNOW THAT ONE OF THE TWO HAD BEEN RIPPED OFF BY THE OTHER. THEY GOT INTO A FIGHT WITH THEIR STONE KNIVES, AND THE MAN WANTING TO DIE, OF COURSE, GOT STABBED TO DEATH BY THE SAID EVIL-MINDED SOUL. AND JUST TO MAKE SURE, THE EVIL-MINDED ONE CUT UP THE OTHER POOR SOUL'S THROAT WITH HIS SOMEWHAT SHARP STONE WEAPON. THIS WAS, OF COURSE, SEEN BY OTHERS SOULS AS JUSTICE BEING

CARRIED OUT TO THE THEIF. BUT THAT VERY SAME NIGHT, THE GHOST OF THE MAN WHO HAD WANTED TO END IT ALL WAS HEARD WALKING ALL OVER THE VILLAGE, SAYING THESE VERY WORDS: "VERY COLD, VERY BAD. I WANT TO BE ALIVE AGAIN. I WANT TO BE ALIVE AGAIN." BUT NO ONE WAS ABLE TO HELP OUT THAT POOR, RECENTLY DEARLY DEPARTED ONE, KNOWING THAT THEY HAD BURIED HIM UNDER THE GROUND ALREADY. SO THIS WAS A VERY BAD MISTAKE OF THAT POOR SOUL. HE HAD TO FIND OUT THAT DYING WAS NOT THE ANSWER FOR ANY GIVEN HARDSHIP OR PROBLEM THAT HAS TO BE FACED EVERYDAY BY MOST LIVING SOULS.

VILLAGERS' REVENGE

THERE WAS THIS OLD WOMAN SOUL WHO HAPPENED TO HAVE A BAD HABIT OF PUBLICLY BALLING OUT HER FELLOW VILLAGE SOULS OF ANYTHING THAT SHE KNEW WERE THEIR SETBACKS OF THEIR DAILY EXISTENCE, IN OUR SOMEWHAT HARD-TO-BE-ALIVE-IN WORLD AND DAILY CHALLENGES THAT WOULD HAVE TO BE OVERCOME, DAY IN AND, NOT TO MENTION, DAY OUT, AND EVERYTHING COMING AROUND IN BETWEEN. SO AS FAR AS EVERYONE KNEW AND HAD ALWAYS KNOWN BEFOREHAND, SHE WAS THE ONE THEY REGRETTED TO HAVE ANY CHANCE OF MEETING HEAD-ON THEIR PATH OF WHEREVER THEY HAPPENED TO BE HEADING. THIS DAILY SCOLDING BY THIS OLD SOUL DID GET ON THE NERVES OF SOME, AND OTHERS AS WELL AS THE OLD, THE MIDDLE AGED, AND ALSO, THE YOUNG VERY MUCH ALIVE LIVING SOULS. WELL THEN, THIS SORT OF A BAD THING OF LETTING OTHERS KNOW WENT ON AND ON FOR QUITE A SPELL--MORE LIKE OVER FIFTY YEARS OR MORE. FOR THIS WAS AN OLD ACTIVE SOUL, WHO WAS KEPT FIT AND HEALTHY BY HER CONSTANT MOVEMENT ACTIVITIES, WHICH SHE WAS INTO VERY MUCH. SO, THAT WAS WHAT KEPT HER GOING

ON A DAY-BY-DAY CONTINUATION, AS SEEN BY OTHERS, AND MUCH TO THE DISAPPOINTMENT AND HURT FEELINGS THAT WERE HEARD, FELT, AND TASTED BY THE OTHER NOT SO VERY STRONG-MINDED LIVING SOULS IN HER VILLAGE'S AREA. BUT SOON, THIS POOR, POOR OLD WOMAN GOT LAID DOWN WITH SICKNESS THAT WAS TO CLAIM HER BODILY GIFT OF HER DAY-BY-DAY EXISTENCE, HERE ON THIS MAKE-IT-AS-WE-SEE-FIT WORLD OF OURS. BUT NOT A SOUL CAME TO HER ASSISTANCE DURING HER TIME OF REMORSE AND FEAR OF THE COMING END OF HER DAILY GIFT OF HER PRECIOUS LIFE NOW COMING ON. NOT TOO LONG AFTER HER SICKNESS HAD LAID HER DOWN FROM HER FORMER VERY ACTIVITY-FILLED DAILY EXISTENCE, SHE GAVE UP THE GHOST AND WAS DEAD, BODILY. FOR NO ONE TRIED TO HELP OR NURSE HER BACK TO HEALTH, DUE TO THE GREAT PRIDE SHE HAD HAD IN BALLING EACH AND EVERY ONE OF THEM OUT. IN HER HOME VILLAGE, WHEN THE LOCALS WERE IN THE PROCESS OF BURNING UP ALL HER EARTHLY WEALTH, SOME OF THE YOUNG MEN DECIDED FOR THEMSELVES THAT THEY WOULD TEACH HER A LESSON BY NOT BURNING UP HER WELL-WORN FUR PARKA, KNOWING BEFOREHAND THAT SHE WOULD BE OUT AND ABOUT IN HER SPIRIT FORM, INQUIRING ABOUT HER VERY MUCH USED OLD PARKA. AFTER GIVING HER A SOMEWHAT DECENT BURIAL, WITHOUT SO

MUCH AS EVEN PLACING THE HEADSTONE OF HER GRAVE TO MARK THE SPOT OF HER BURIAL SITE OUT IN THE WILDERNESS AWAY FROM THEIR EXISTING BURIAL GROUNDS FOR FORMERLY VERY ALIVE SOULS, THE YOUNG MEN THEN WAITED VERY PATIENTLY FOR HER SPIRIT TO COME OUT AND DO SOME SCOLDING AND, NOT TO MENTION, FUSSING. AS SOON AS THE YOUNG SOULS HEARD HER BALLING OUT EVERYONE-YES, EVEN THE DOGS, WE SUPPOSE--THEY THREW HER PARKA INTO THE FIRE JUST TO SEE WHAT WOULD HAPPEN. AS SOON AS THEY HAD DONE SO, THE POOR OLD SOUL'S SPIRIT STARTED CRYING AND APOLOGIZING REALLY LOUDLY ABOUT HER PAST. AFTER SEEING THAT SHE WAS SUFFERING ERCATLY, THE VILLAGERS FORGAVE HER RIGHT AWAY, KNOWING THAT SHE WAS IN GREAT AGONY, AND THAT GREAT PAIN WAS FELT BY HER VERY ALIVE SPIRIT OR SOUL.

THE BOY BORN WITH A BIG MOUTH

THIS YOUNG WOMAN WAS PREGNANT, AND WOULD SOON HAVE HER HELP AROUND THE HOUSE, WHICH SHE NEEDED VERY MUCH, AND WAS HOPING FOR QUITE SOON, FOR SHE WAS WITH CHILD, DESPITE THE FACT THAT SHE DID NOT HAVE A HUSBAND. HER MAN HAD BEEN TAKEN AWAY FROM HER BY BODILY DEATH, WHICH IS VERY MERCILESS AND DOES NOT CARE FOR ALL LIVING SOULS. NOT VERY LONG AGO, SHE KNEW BY THE SIZE OF HER STOMACH, WHICH BORE THE YET UNBORN LITTLE BABY SOUL THAT IT WOULD DEFINITELY NOT BE SUCH A LONG TIME TO WAIT BEFORE ITS BIRTH OUT TO THIS VERY GOOD WORLD OF OURS, CALLED EARTH. ONE NIGHT, AS SHE WAS IN HER LABOR PAINS, ONE OF HER FELLOW WOMAN SOULS CAME TO HER PLACE, SO THAT SHE COULD ASSIST HER IN HER TIME OF NEEDING SOMEONE ELSE'S ASSISTANCE. THE LABORING PART DID LAST QUITE A SPELL, WITH BOTH THE WOMAN AND HER SOULFUL HELP BREAKING OUT IN BIG SWEATS DURING THE ONGOING LABOR PAINS. BUT FINALLY, THE NEWLY BORN BABY SOUL WAS AMONG THE ALIVE AND WELL. THE MAID HELPER WHISKED HIM OFF TO CLEAN HIM UP

RIGHT AWAY AFTER IT WAS BORN, AND IT WAS A LITTLE BOY. SHE MANAGED TO TELL THE MOTHER, WHEN SHE ASKED THE MAID TO SEE HER NEWBORN LITTLE SON, TO WAIT A WHILE LONGER, BUT WOULD NOT BRING HIM TO HER, FOR HER TO SEE FOR HERSELF. AFTER SOME TIME HAD PASSED, SHE AGAIN REQUESTED, WANTING TO SEE HER BABY BOY SOUL, AND YET RECEIVED THE SAME REPLY, THAT SHE COULD NOT SEE HIM JUST YET. SO SHE DOZED OFF TO SLEEP, TO REST IN HER TIREDNESS FROM BRINGING A CHILD SOUL OUT TO OUR WORLD. WHEN SHE FINALLY WOKE UP DURING THE LATE EVENING HOURS, SHE TOLD THE MAID THAT SHE WANTED TO SEE HER BABY AGAIN. AFTER SEEING THAT THE MOM WAS VERY SERIOUS THIS TIME AROUND, SHE RELUCTANTLY BROUGHT HER THE NEW BOY SOUL FOR HER TO SEE. WHAT SHE SAW SHOCKED THE MOTHER GREATLY, WHEN SHE SAW THAT THE BOY HAD A MOUTH THAT STARTED FROM ONE EAR, AND THE LENGTH OF HIS YOUNG MOUTH REACHED THE OTHER EAR, ON THE OTHER SIDE OF HIS SMALL HEAD. BUT THE YOUNG MOTHER DECIDED FOR HERSELF, AFTER SEEING HER BIG-MOUTHED SON, THAT SHE WOULD RAISE HIM AND LOVE HIM AS HER VERY OWN, DESPITE HIS VERY DIFFERENT APPEARANCE. WHEN THE BOY WAS A YOUNG CHILD, ALL THE OTHER CHILDREN SOULS MADE GREAT FUN OF HIM, WHICH MADE THE YOUNG CHILD QUITE MAD,

AND MADE HIM FEEL WORTHLESS AND ALL THE BAD STUFF. HE, OF COURSE, BLAMED ALL HIS CURRENT SETBACKS ON HIS DEAR OLD MOTHER, AND HE WOULD OFTEN TELL HER THAT HE WOULD KILL HER AND EAT HER UP VERY SOON. THE MOM ONLY THOUGHT OF IT AS LOOSE-TONGUE TALK, BUT ONE FATEFUL DAY, THE BIG-MOUTHED YOUNG SOUL DID CARRY OUT HIS THREATS AGAINST HIS POOR OLD MOTHER. THE YOUNG SOUL SOMEHOW KILLED HIS MOTHER AND ATE SOME PART OF HER FACE. WHEN THE LOCALS FOUND OUT WHAT HAD TAKEN PLACE, THEY TOOK THE POOR BIG-MOUTHED BOY OUT, AND CLUBBED HIM TO DEATH, USING THEIR BIG SEAL-KILLING CLUBS. AFTER HE HAD DIED, THEY DID NOT BOTHER TO BURY HIM, BUT RATHER, BURNED UP HIS SMALL BODY, WITH CLEAR THOUGHTS THAT ALL EVIL WOULD BE BURNED UP ALONG WITH HIM, AND NOT EVER OCCUR AGAIN IN THEIR SMALL VILLAGE.

WAS LEG BONE

THESE TWO SMALL CHILDREN SOULS WERE OUT PLAYING HIDE-AND-SEEK ONE DAY. THE AREA THAT THEY WERE ENJOYING THEIR ACTIVITIES, WHICH WERE VERY MUCH FUN FOR THAT DAY, WAS IN A CERTAIN GRASSY AREA NOT TOO FAR FROM THEIR HOME VILLAGE, WHERE JUST THE TWO OF THEM HAD BEEN OUT AT SINCE THE EARLY MORNING HOURS. AND THEY HAD WITH THEM A SMALL DOG, WITH WHICH THEY TOOK TURNS LOCATING THE ONE THAT WAS HIDING, DUE TO THE REAL FACT THAT THE DOG WAS EASILY ABLE TO SNIFF OUT AND THEREFORE FIND THE OTHER SMALL SOUL, WHEREVER HE MAY BE HIDDEN DURING THEIR MUCH FUN-FILLED GAME. IT LASTED UNTIL ABOUT NOONTIME. THAT WAS WHEN THE USUAL HUNGRY TIME WAS ON OPERATION INSIDE THEIR SMALL, EASILY FILLED-UP STOMACHES. AND BOTH OF THESE VERY MUCH ALIVE AND LIVELY YOUNG SOULS WERE JUST ABOUT GETTING ON THE WEAKENED SIDE, DUE TO NOT HAVING EATEN SINCE THE TIME THAT THEY HAD EATEN THEIR BREAKFASTS EARLY THAT SAME MORNING. WELL THEN, ON THEIR LAST FIND OF THEIR HIDE-AND-GO-SEEK GAME, ONE OF OTHERS,

THE ONE THAT WAS HIDING, HAPPENED TO STUMBLE ACROSS A PIECE OF BIG BONE, WHICH HE HAPPENED TO HAVE A LIKING FOR RIGHT OFF THE BAT. HE THEREFORE DECIDED FOR HIMSELF THAT HE WOULD HAVE IT FOR HIMSELF, AND THOUGHT OUT PLANS SINCE HE NOW HAD A CLUB THAT HE COULD USE WHENEVER THE NEED FOR ITS USE HAPPENED TO ARRIVE, SOMETIME IN HIS FUTURE DAYS. SO HE HID IT ON THE INSIDE SECTION OF HIS SOMEWHAT OVERSIZED PARKA, SO THAT NO ONE WOULD SEE IT AND THEREFORE TAKE IT AWAY FROM HEM ON THEIR WAY HOME. HE MADE SURE THAT IT DID NOT HAVE A CHANCE TO SLIP OUT FROM HIS PARKA, SO HE HELD ONTO IT QUITE TIGHTLY. WHEN HE GOT TO HIS HOUSE, HE HID IT BY BURYING IT ALONG THE SIDE OF HIS HOUSE, WENT TO HIS PARENTS' HOME, AND HAD HIS LUNCH, WHICH HE WAS QUITE FAMISHED FOR. AFTERWARDS, HE THOUGHT TO HIMSELF THAT HE WAS GOING TO USE THE NEWLY-ACQUIRED BIG PIECE OF BONE AS A CLUB, TO CLUB WHATEVER NEEDED TO BE CLUBBED BY THE SMALL CHILD SOUL HIMSELF. HE GAVE NO FURTHER THOUGHT OF THE THING IN QUESTION FOR THE DURATION OF THAT SAME OLD DAY, BUT EARLY THE FOLLOWING MORNING, BIG NEWS WAS BEING CIRCULATED--BY WORD OF MOUTH, OF COURSE--THAT THERE HAD BEEN SOMETHING WANDERING AROUND THAT SMALL SOUL'S VILLAGE THAT WAS

LOOKING FOR HIS LEG. WHEN THE SMALL SOUL'S MOTHER HAPPENED TO BREAK THE BIG NEWS TO HER HOUSEHOLD, THE SMALL THOUGHTFUL YOUNG CHILD REMEMBERED WHAT HE HAD FOUND IN A CERTAIN GRASSY AREA THE DAY BEFORE. SO HE SHOWED THE BIG PIECE OF BONE TO HIS MOTHER, WHO SAW THAT IT WAS A PIECE OF A FORMERLY ALIVE MAN OR WOMAN'S LEG BONE. THAT WAS WHEN THE MOM REALIZED THAT WAS WHAT THAT LEG-SEARCHING SPIRIT WAS LOOKING FOR THE OTHER NIGHT. SO SHE HAD HER SON SHOW HER WHERE IT WAS RETRIEVED FROM, AND BOTH SHE AND HER SMALL CHILD LIVING SOUL WENT BACK TO THE VERY SAME SPOT AND REBURIED IT AT THE VERY SAME SPOT FROM WHICH IT HAD BEEN TAKEN BY THAT SMALL SOUL BOY.

THREE NIGHT VISITORS

THIS BAD SOUL, WHO LOVED TO CARRY OUT BAD THINGS, WAS LYING ON HIS BED, TAKING IT EASY, THINKING ABOUT NOTHING BUT BAD THOUGHTS THAT HE STILL WANTED TO DO IN HIS FUTURE GIFT OF HIS DAILY EXISTENCE. HE THOUGHT ABOUT DOING WHAT HE DID KNOW HOW TO DO VERY EASILY, AND WAS NOT EVEN A BIT SORRY FOR ALL THE THINGS--ALL BAD, OF COURSE--THAT HE HAD COMMITTED IN TIMES AND DAYS ALREADY PAST. WELL THEN, HE WAS DOING HIS FAVORITE THING, AND THAT WAS DOING SOME SERIOUS THOUGHT WORKOUT, WHEN HE THOUGHT THAT HE HEARD SOME PEOPLE TALKING OUT ON HIS PORCH, BUT THEY WERE SO MUFFLED THAT NOTHING COULD BE UNDERSTOOD BY THE BAD-DEEDS-LOVING SOUL HIMSELF. SO HE CHECKED OUT HIS PORCH, BUT WHAT HE SAW WAS THAT NO ONE WAS EVEN AROUND ON HIS VERY MUCH EMPTY PORCH. SO HE THEREFORE GAVE IT NO MORE THOUGHT FOR THE DURATION OF THAT SAME EVENING. THE FOLLOWING DAY, AFTER THIS SAID BAD SOUL WAS DOING HIS MUCH LOVED ACTIVITY (DOING SOME THOUGHT WORK IN HIS NOT-SO-STRAIGHTENED-OUT HEAD ON

TOP OF HIS LYING AROUND AREA) HE AGAIN
HEARD SOME VOICES OUT ON HIS PORCH'S
LOCATION YET AGAIN, THE SAME AS ON THE
PRECEDING DAY. BUT WHEN HE CHECKED IT
OUT, THE VERY SAME STORY PLAYED OUT ON
HIS PORCH: THAT IS, NOT A SOUL WAS TO BE
SEEN ANYWHERE ON HIS HOUSE'S PORCH. ON
THE THIRD EVENING OF THESE INDEED VERY
WEIRD THINGS GOING ON, VERY MUCH TO THE
DISLIKE OF THAT VERY BAD SOUL, THIS TIME
AROUND, HE DECIDED FOR HIMSELF THAT HE
WOULD WAIT OUT THOSE MUFFLED VOICES
THAT HE HAD BEEN HEARING IN HIS MUCH
LIVED-IN LIVING ROOM AND KITCHEN AREA.
HE WAS NOT A BIT SURPRISED WHEN THOSE
VOICES STARTED TO TALK SOMETHING OUT,
YET AGAIN FROM HIS PORCH. AND THIS TIME,
THERE WAS A KNOCK ON HIS DOORWAY, AND
HE, THE BAD SOUL, NOT BEING A SCARED BAD
SOUL, TOLD THE KNOCKER TO COME RIGHT
IN. THERE WERE THREE OF THEM, AND ONE
OF THOSE THREE SOULS WAS A WOMAN.
THESE THREE HAD BLACKENED LEATHERY
SKIN, AND ROT WAS ON THEM, ALSO. AND
THEY SMELLED VERY BAD, INDEED. THE THREE
VERY LOST SOULS DID NOT SAY ANYTHING AT
FIRST, BUT THEN, AFTER SOME TIME HAD PAST,
ONE OF THE LOST, BAD-SMELLING SPIRITS
FINALLY TOLD THE BAD SOUL THAT THEY
HAD BEEN SENT BY THE MOST EVIL-MINDED
DEVIL TO ASK HIM IF THEY COULD POSSESS
HIM. THEY PROMISED HIM THAT IF HE DID NOT

LIKE IT, THEY WOULD LEAVE HIS BODY AND SPIRIT IMMEDIATLY ON HIS SAY-SO. THAT GOT THIS BAD SOUL VERY SCARED ON THE SPOT, WHEN THEY TOLD HIM THAT, AND TOLD HIM TO THINK ABOUT THE MATTER, ALSO. THEY ALSO TOLD HIM THAT THEY WOULD GUIDE HIM OR HELP HIM CARRY OUT HIS BAD DEEDS, IF HE GAVE THEM THE OKAY TO POSSESS HIS BODY AND SPIRIT. WHEN THEY FINALLY LEFT HIS HOUSE, THE BAD SOUL CONTACTED THE VILLAGE PRIEST AND HAD HIM REMOVE THE HEX FROM HIS HOUSE, AFTER TELLING HIM THE WHOLE STORY. AFTERWARDS, THIS MAN SOUL CHANGED HIS BAD WAYS AND STARTED DOING AND BEING GOOD, AFTER THOSE VISITING LOST SPIRITS, WITH VERY BAD ODORS ALL AROUND THEM, HAD PAID HIM A NOT-SO-GOOD VISIT. THEY SEEMED TO HAVE BEEN BURNED UP BY A VERY HOT FIRE SOMEWHERE.

DEMONS ARE ALWAYS ABOUT

THIS BAD-DEEDS-LOVING SOUL WAS LIVING IN THIS SMALL VILLAGE AND THE ACTIVITY OF THIS NOT-SO-GOOD MAN WAS TO BE OUT LATE AT NIGHT, AND ALSO IN THE VERY EARLY MORNING HOURS, WHILE THE REST OF THE VILLAGE SLEPT. HE DID WHAT HE HAPPENED TO START UP DOING NOT VERY LONG AGO, BUT QUITE RECENTLY, LIKE MAYBE A WEEK OR SO AGO. AND THE ACTIVITY THAT WAS TAKEN CARE OF BY THIS BAD SOUL WAS TO DO SOME SERIOUS MISCHIEF, WHICH HE, THE BAD-DEEDS-LOVING SOUL CARRIED OUT NIGHTLY. WELL, WHAT HE DID WAS QUITE BAD, ACCORDING TO THE VILLAGERS HE WAS LIVING WITH, BUT THEY HAD NO IDEA WHO HAD BEEN UNTYING THEIR SLED LEGGINGS, AND ALSO, THE DOGS OF THESE OTHER SOULS HAD BEEN MOVED OR HAD BEEN SWITCHED AROUND--THAT IS, THE DOGS HAD BEEN MOVED TO OTHER DOG CHAINS' TIE-UP POST SITES. IN ORDER TO MAKE A LONG STORY SHORT, HE WAS UP TO NO GOOD ON A NIGHTLY BASIS, BUT WOULD SOON CHANGE AFTER HIS CHANCE MEETING WITH TWO UGLY LITTLE DEMONS WHO WERE TRYING TO DO HIM HARM, SO THAT THEY COULD TAKE HIS

SPIRIT AND TORTURE HIS SOUL BY USING
A VERY HOT FIRE SOMEWHERE. ON THAT
FATEFUL DAY, THIS YOUNG SOUL WHO LOVED
TO DO BAD DEEDS WAS ON HIS WAY BACK
TO HIS HOUSE, AFTER MUCH MISCHIEF HAD
BEEN CARRIED OUT BY HIM. WELL THEN, HE
WAS FEELING PRETTY GOOD ABOUT HAVING
MESSED UP A LOT ON THAT FATEFUL DAY.
FOR HIM, SATISFACTION WAS IN HIS MISLEAD
MIND, AND HE WAS QUITE HAPPY THAT HIS
FELLOW SOULS WOULD NOT BE TOO HAPPY
WHEN THEY GOT UP EARLY THAT SAME
MORNING. AS FAR AS WE KNOW, HE WAS
ON HIS WAY TO HIS PLACE, WHEN HE HAD A
HEAD-ON MEEETING WITH THESE HAIRY AND
VERY FOUL-ODORED, UGLY DEMONS. AND
THESE TWO VERY EVIL CREATURES WERE IN A
VERY FOUL MOOD, MEANING THAT THEY WERE
VERY MAD, INDEED. AND WHEN THEY MET THE
POOR BAD SOUL, ALL THEY SAID WAS THIS
VERY QUOTE: "SO YOU ARE THE ONE THAT
HAS BEEN DOING THE BAD DEEDS THAT WE
DID HAVE GREAT INTENTIONS OF CARRYING
OUT." AFTER SAYING THIS, THE EVIL SPIRITS
GRABBED THE POOR BAD SOUL TO HIS FEET
AND DRAGGED HIM TO A NEARBY HILL, ON
WHICH THEY THEN DID SOL, DESPITE HIS
STRUGGLES TO BE FREE OF THEIR SOMEWHAT
FIRM GRIP ON HIS FEET. WHEN THEY GOT TO
THE SIDE OF THAT SAID SMALL HILL, THEY
OPENED UP AN INVISIBLE DOORWAY ON THE
SIDE OF THE HILL. AND THEY WERE PULLING

HIM, THE BAD SOUL, RIGHT IN TO THAT PLACE, WHICH MIGHT HAVE BEEN HIS BURIAL SITE, IF THEY HAD ONLY SUCCEEDED IN DOING SO. BUT SOMETHING KEPT THESE TWO EVIL SPIRITS FROM SUCCEEDING IN WHATEVER THEY HAD BEEN TRYING TO DO, WHICH WAS TO PULL THIS POOR BAD SOUL THROUGH THAT FORMERLY INVISIBLE DOORWAY. SOMEWHERE ALONG THE WAY, THE BAD MAN HAPPENED TO PASS OUT FROM ALL THIS EVIL COMMOTION TAKING PLACE. WHEN HE CAME TO, IT WAS ALREADY DAYLIGHT, AND THE SUN WAS UP HIGH IN THE BLUE SKY, AND THE BAD MAN WAS STILL VERY ALIVE AND WELL. WHEN HE HAPPENED TO CHECK THINGS OUT, HE FOUND OUT THAT HIS SOMEWHAT LONG HAIR HAD SNAGGED ON A SMALL TWIG, AND THAT SMALL TWIG HAD THEREFORE SAVED HIS DAILY GIFT OF LIFE FROM THOSE MAD SMALL DEMONS, WHO HAD EVIL INTENTIONS ONLY, AND WERE VERY BAD-SMELLING, WITH ROTTED-OUT FACES. LATER, FROM THAT DAY ON, THIS ONE WAS A SOUL WHO CHANGED HIS WAYS, AND WAS REALLY INTO MAKING STUFF THAT HE COULD GIVE AWAY, FOR USE BY HIS FELLOW VILLAGE SOULS. HE, THE FORMERLY BAD MAN, KNEW THEY WOULD BE OF GREAT HELP TO THEM, AND WHAT THEY DID ON A DAILY BASIS.

MAN'S ONLY LIFE GIVEN

THERE WAS A FAMINE GOING ON, IN THE LIVING, DAILY GIFTS OF OUR VERY PRECIOUS LIVES, AROUND THE VERY MUCH ALIVE SOULS WHO JUST HAPPENED TO CONSIST OF THE PARENTS AND THEIR VERY YOUNG DAUTHER. THESE THREE LIVING SOULS HAPPENED TO BE AWAY FROM THEIR HOME VILLAGE, KNOWING THAT THEY HAD A BETTER CHANCE OF LIVING OUT THE RELENTLESS AND VERY MERCILESS ONGOING SHORTAGE OF FOOD, WHICH WOULD THEREFORE MAKE THESE LIVING SOULS VERY HUNGRY THAT WINTER, WHICH WAS FAST APPROACHING THE AREA AS A WHOLE. SO, THE MOTHER AND WIFE, ONE DAY, DECIDED FOR HERSELF THAT SHE WOULD DO SOME BEACH-COMBING IN HOPES OF FINDING SOME ANIMAL, OR FISH, FOR THAT MATTER, ON HER PATH ON THE BEACH AREA THAT SHE HAPPENED TO BE WALKING ON. SOON, IN THE DISTANCE, AND IN THE DIRECTION THAT SHE HAPPENED TO BE WALKING, SHE DID SEE SOMETHING WHITE. IT SEEMED TO BE ANOTHER SOUL, DOING SOMETHING TO THAT WHITE OBJECT. WHEN SHE GOT CLOSE ENOUGH TO SEE AND RECOGNIZE THIS SOMETHING, SHE SAW, WITH HER OWN EYES, THAT IT WAS AN IMP, AN

EVIL LITTLE SPIRIT CUTTING UP A FRESHLY-KILLED BELUGA WHALE. WHEN THE FEMALE SOUL ASKED FOR SOME MEAT FROM THAT LITTLE EVIL CREATURE, THE IMP DID NOT EVEN LOOK UP, BUT KEPT CUTTING UP THE WHALE WITH HIS SOMEWHAT SMALL AND VERY SHARP KNIFE. BUT THE WOMAN KEPT UP HER REQUEST FOR SOME OF THAT FRESH MEAT, WHICH SHE KNEW WOULD HELP OUT A LOT, FOOD-WISE, DURING THAT ONGOING FAMINE OF THE LAND. AFTER THE WOMAN (WHO WAS ALSO A WIFE) ASKED FOR SOME MEAT FOR ABOUT THE TENTH TIME, THE LITTLE EVIL SPIRIT TOLD HER IN HIS SOMEWHAT EVIL-SOUNDING VOICE THAT THERE WAS A VERY HIGH PRICE FOR HIS WHALE MEAT. BUT HE WOULD NOT TELL HER WHAT THE PRICE FOR HIS FRESHLY KILLED WHALE MEAT WAS. SO, SHE KEPT ASKING WHAT THE PRICE MAY THEREFORE BE. FINALLY, THE EVIL SPIRIT TOLD HER THAT IF SHE REALLY WANTED THE WHALE, THE LIFE OF ONE OF HER LOVED ONES WAS TO BE TRADED FOR THE WHALE. HE TOLD HER ALL THIS WITH A VERY SAD-LOOKING EVIL LITTLE FACE. THE WOMAN PLAYED ALONG, FOR SHE DID NOT THINK THAT THE THING WAS EVEN SERIOUS. SO SHE TOLD HIM THAT HER HUSBAND'S LIFE WOULD BE GIVEN FOR THE WHALE. THEN, THE LITTLE EVIL SPIRIT SHOOK HER HAND, AND THEREFORE TOLD HER IT WAS A DEAL. THEN, HE GOT INTO HIS LONG KAYAK AND TOOK OFF

INTO THE SEA, NEVER TO BE SEEN AGAIN BY THIS FOOD-WANTING SOUL. HER FAMILY WAS VERY SURPRISED WHEN SHE BROUGHT SOME OF THE MEAT THAT SAME EVENING, BUT SHE DID NOT TELL ANYONE WHAT THE LITTLE EVIL SPIRIT HAD TOLD HER--THAT A LIFE WOULD HAVE TO BE TAKEN--FOR SHE THOUGHT TO HERSELF THAT ALL WOULD BE WELL. BUT EARLY THE NEXT MORNING, SHE TRIED TO WAKE HER MAN UP, AND HE WAS NOT EVEN RESPONDING TO HER WISHES. SHE FOUND OUT THAT HE HAD DIED SOMETIME DURING THE NIGHT. THEN, IT GOT INTO HER SOUL VERY DEEPLY THAT THE PRICE FOR THAT WHALE MEAT HAD BEEN AGREED UPON: THE LIFE OF HER VERY MUCH LOVED AND APPRECIATED DEAR, DEAR FORMER HUSBAND, WHO WAS SOMEPLACE IN HIS SPIRIT FORM, AND VERY MUCH STILL ALIVE IN SPIRIT.

GRAVEYARD HAND

THERE WERE THESE TWO SMALL AND YOUNG MISCHIEVOUS SOULS, WHO WERE QUITE YOUNG, VERY ALIVE, AND ACTIVE, WHO HAPPENED TO BE BUDDIES AND ALL. BUT THE DOWN SIDE OF THEM LIVING OUT THEIR DAILY GIFTS OF BEING VERY ALIVE AND ALSO WELL, WHICH WAS CARRIED OUT BY THESE SMALL SOULS, WAS THAT THEY HAD A VERY BAD HABIT. AND THE BAD THAT THEY DID WAS QUITE A NIGHTMARE, AS FAR AS THE WHOLE VILLAGE DID SEE, BUT THEY DID NOT HAVE ANY KNOWLEDGE OF WHO HAD BEEN CARRYING OUT OR CREATING HAVOC IN THE VILLAGE'S PLACEMENT OF THE BODILY DEAD. AS FAR AS EVERYONE KNEW, THE HEAD LOCATION MARKERS DID HAVE BIG PROBLEMS, BEING KNOCKED DOWN, AND SOMETIMES, THE VILLAGE DOGS WOULD BE TIED UP TO THE MARKER POLES ON A SOMEWHAT REGULAR BASIS. AND THE GIFTS THAT HAD BEEN OFFERED WOULD OFTEN BE EATEN BY THESE, WHO WERE NOT-SO-WELL, HEAD-WISE. WELL THEN, THE TWO (AS FAR AS WE KNOW) SMALL BAD SOULS DID HAVE A DATE SCHEDULED THAT WOULD SCARE THEM UP REALLY WELL, AND PUT AN END TO THEIR DAILY BAD DEEDS. FOR A

FORMER POWERFUL SHAMAN, ONE OF THOSE
THAT HAD HELPED A LOT OF SICK SOULS GET
WELL AND, NOT TO MENTION, HAD POWERFUL
MEDICINE FOR ALL TYPES OF DISEASE AND
THE SICKNESS ALSO INCLUDED, DIED BODILY.
JUST TO MAKE A LONG STORY SHORT, A LOT
OF GOODIES WERE OFFERED TO THE GROUND
BURIAL SITE OF THIS FORMER SERVENT OF
SATAN, THE HATER OF ALL MANKIND, AND
SELF-CENTERED OLD FOOL. AND ALSO, HE
IS THE KING OF NOTHING. ANYWAY, WHAT
THESE TWO FOOLISH YOUNG SOULS DID
RIGHT AFTER THE PASSING OF THAT FORMER
SHAMAN WAS SOME GRAVEYARD VISITING,
JUST TO CARRY OUT THEIR CHOICE OF THE
DAILY BAD DEEDS THAT THEY HAD BEEN UP
TO FOR QUITE SOME TIME. WELL, THEY WERE
LOOKING OVER THAT LOSER'S FORMER
SERVANT'S BURIAL SITE, AND SAW ALL THE
GOODIES THAT THE GRATEFUL SOULS HAD
GIVEN. THEY THEREFORE STARTED THEIR
MESSING-UP BUSINESS AT THAT SITE. BUT
BEFORE TOO LONG, AN EVIL DEMON'S HAND
SURFACED FROM BELOW GROUND AND
GRABBED AND HELD ON TO ONE OF THESE
SMALL SOULS DOING BAD DEEDS. THEY DID
A LOT TO THAT EVIL DEMON'S CLAW. THEY
CLUBBED IT WITH SOME OF THE HEAD LOCATOR
POLES. THEY KICKED IT WITH THEIR SMALL
FEET. ALL THE WHILE, THEY WERE ALSO
SHOCKED, KNOWING THAT SOMETHING OF
THIS MAGNATUDE HAD NEVER OCCURRED IN

THEIR PAST GRAVEYARD-MESSING-AROUND ACTIVITIES. FINALLY, ONE OF BOYS OUT OF THE BLUE ACCIDENTLY DROOLED SOME OF HIS SALIVA ON THE HAND OF THE EVIL, CLAWED DEMON, WHO WAS OUT TO DO NOT GOOD. WHEN THE SALIVA CAME IN CONTACT WITH THE EVIL HAND THAT HAD APPEARED FROM THE BURIAL SITE OF THAT FORMER SERVANT OF THE MOST EVIL SPIRIT OF THEM ALL, IT STARTED SMOKING AND IMMEDIATELY LET GO OF THE SMALL SOUL'S LEG. ALSO, SOME LOUD SCREAMS WERE HEARD BY THESE YOUNG SOULS, AS THE EVIL HAND DISAPPEARED ONCE AND FOR ALL BELOW GROUND. THE POOR SOULS THEN RAN HOME, CRYING AND SHOUTING UNCONTROLLABLY. AND AFTERWARDS, THEY NO LONGER SHOWED DISRESPECT TO THE LOCAL PLACEMENT AREA OF THOSE THAT WERE NO LONGER AROUND BODILY.

WAS MUKLUK SHOE

AN OLD WOMAN SOUL HAD DIED VERY RECENTLY, AND THE RELATIVES OF THIS ROCK-OLD SOUL THEREFORE MADE ALL THE PREPARATIONS FOR HER BURIAL, AND MADE SURE THAT SOME FOODS THAT WERE TRADITIONAL FOR HER PASSING WERE COOKED UP AND WERE READIED FOR THE UPCOMING FEAST, WHICH WAS TO TAKE PLACE IN HER SMALL HOME VILLAGE, AS WAS CUSTOM. THE RELATIVES OF THE RECENTLY DECEASED DID SO, AS HAD BEEN CARRIED OUT FOR HUNDREDS OR PERHAPS THOUSANDS OF YEARS BEFORE THESE SAID GOOD SOUL RELATIVES (OR PERHAPS BAD SOUL RELATIVES) DID ALL THEY COULD TO MAKE SURE THAT THE OLD DEAD BODY WOULD HAVE A SOMEWHAT DECENT PLACE MENT IN THE UNDERSIDE OF OUR SOMETIMES HARD-TO-DEAL WITH DIRT-COVERED HOME. WELL, THESE SAID RELATIVES MADE SURE THAT ALL OF THIS OLD SOUL'S CLOTHES WERE BURNED, AND THERE FORE, DESTROYED BY USE OF A FIRE. AND ANYTHING THAT WAS NOT CAPABLE OF BURNING UP WAS PLACED INSIDE HER COFFIN. AFTER ALL HAD BEEN SAID AND DONE, THINGS SEEMED TO GO WELL FOR ALL THESE

SOULS, BUT WOULD DRASTICALLY CHANGE THE VERY SAME NIGHT THAT THE POOR, POOR OLD SOUL'S BODY HAD BEEN BURIED VERY DECENTLY BELOW THE HEARTLESS FROZEN GROUND. WELL, IT TOOK PLACE THAT VERY SAME EVENING THAT THE RESTLESS LOST SPIRIT OF THAT OLD SOUL APPEARED ON SOME PORCH, AND COULD BE HEARD OUT ON THE PORCH AS IF SHE WAS SEARCHING FOR SOMETHING. AND THIS SEARCHING FOR WHATEVER WOULD LAST AT LEAST A WEEK OR SO, UNTIL THESE RELATIVES THAT HAD BEEN LEFT BEHIND GOT REALLY FED UP, AND THEIR SLEEP PATTERNS WERE GREATLY DISORIENTED AND OUT OF PLACE, DUE TO THE CONTINUAL PORCH NOISES. FINALLY, ONE OF THE SOULS THAT WAS STILL ALIVE BODILY AND SPIRITUALLY DECIDED THAT HE WOULD HAVE A LOOK AT WHAT WAS ON THEIR HOME'S PORCH. WHAT HE FOUND OUT THAT DAY WAS THAT THE SPIRIT THAT WAS LOST FOREVER HAD BEEN LOOKING FOR ONE PAIR OF HER MUKLUK SHOES, WHICH HAPPENED TO HAVE BEEN LEFT ALONE WHEN ALL THE OTHER ARTICLES OF STUFF TO BE BURNED HAD BEEN CARRIED OUT. SO THIS SOUL, THEREFORE, TOOK THIS LEFT BEHIND MUKLUK SHOE OUT TO THE BURNING AREA, FILLED THE MUKLUK SHOE FULL OF THE BURNABLE AVAILABLE SEAL OIL, AND BURNED IT UP THAT DAY. THE FOLLOWING DAYS THAT CAME WENT QUITE WELL FOR THE RELATIVES OF THAT SPIRIT

SEARCHING FOR MUKLUK SHOES, AND THEY NO LONGER HEARD ANYTHING OUT IN THEIR PORCH AREA, AFTER THE POOR, POOR LOST SPIRIT'S MUKLUK SHOE HAD BEEN DESTROYED WITH THE USE OF SEAL OIL TO BURN IT UP.

LIAR'S REWARD

THESE TWO SOULS, VERY ALIVE INDEED, WERE OUT IN THE WOODED AREA AWAY FROM THEIR HOME VILLAGE ONE DAY. THESE TWO, CONSISTING OF A MAN AND, OF COURSE, HIS WIFE, WHOM HE DID LOVE VERY MUCH SO, HAPPENED TO BE OUT IN THAT IMMEDIATE AREA ON A WOOD-GATHERING MISSION. WHILE THEY GOT DEEPER INTO THE WOODED AREA AWAY FROM THE RIVER, THEY HAPPENED TO SEE A LITTLE EVIL DEMON SLICING UP A FRESHLY KILLED MOOSE. AND THAT LITTLE EVIL-FACED DEMON WITH A MOUTH FROM EAR TO EAR AND, OF COURSE, COVERED WITH SOME UNIDENTIFIED HAIR, HAD SHARP FANGS COMING FROM HIS UPPER LIP AND TWO FANGS ALSO SHOWED FROM HIS EVIL LOWER LIP AREA. THIS LITTLE EVIL CREATURE WAS NOT PAYING MUCH ATTENTION TO HIS IMMEDIATE SURROUNDINGS, AS IF HE WAS EXPECTING NOTHING OUT OF THE ORDINARY TO POP UP FOR HIM, THE LITTLE EVIL-FACED DEMON. WHEN THE TWO VERY MUCH ALIVE LIVING SOULS CAME WITHIN ABOUT TEN FEET OR SO, THE MAN SOFTLY WHISTLED. THIS, OF COURSE, STARTLED THE LITTLE EVIL DEMON AND MADE HIM DROP HIS SOMEWHAT SHARP

LITTLE KNIFE. HE LOOKED AT THE MAN AND HIS WIFE, QUITE EVIL OF SURPRISE. AFTER BEING QUIET FOR A MINUTE OR SO, THE MAN HAPPENED TO ASK THE LITTLE EVIL-FACED CREATURE SPIRIT FOR SOME OF HIS FRESHLY KILLED MOOSE MEAT. WHEN THIS WAS TOLD TO THAT SMALL EVIL SPIRIT, HE SEEMED TO BE IN DEEP THOUGHT FOR ONLY A MOMENT. HE TOLD THEM THAT THEY COULD HAVE THE WHOLE MOOSE MEAT ON ONLY ONE CONDITION. AND THAT WAS THAT NEITHER OF THEM WAS TO TAKE CREDIT FOR THE KILLING OF THAT MOOSE. BOTH THE MAN AND HIS WIFE FULLY AGREED THAT THEY WOULD NOT LIE OR ANYTHING OF THE SORT AGAINST THE LITTLE EVIL SPIRIT. BEFORE HE TOOK OFF INTO THE WOODS, THE SMALL EVIL CREATURE TOLD THEM THAT SOMETHING EVIL WOULD HAPPEN IF THEY DID ANY LYING AND CLAIMED FOR THEMSELVES THAT THEY HAD KILLED THAT MOOSE THAT DAY. AFTER ALL HAD BEEN SAID AND DONE, THESE TWO LYING SOULS WERE FULL OF STORIES ABOUT HOW THE MAN HAD KILLED THAT MOOSE AND THE WIFE BACKED UP HIS LIES WITH ALL HER HEART. BACK IN THEIR HOME VILLAGE, THESE TWO CASHED THE FRESH MEAT IN THEIR SMALL MEAT STORAGE BUILDING, AND HAD A BIG DINNER OF THAT TASTY MOOSE THAT VERY SAME EVENING. THE FOLLOWING DAY, THEY WERE QUITE A BIT SURPRISED WHEN THEY WENT OUT TO THEIR SMALL MEAT STORAGE

BUILDING AND FOUND OUT THAT THE MOOSE MEAT WAS NO LONGER FRESH, BUT WAS FULL OF MAGGOTS, AND THE MEAT'S COLOR WAS NO LONGER FRESH RED, BUT WAS GREEN, AND FULL OF BAD ODORS. THEN, THEY REMEMBERED WHAT THE EVIL SMALL CREATURE HAD TOLD THEM: THAT SOMETHING EVIL AWAITED THEM IF THEY CLAIMED TO HAVE KILLED THAT MOOSE BY THEMSELVES. THEIR LYING HAD DONE THEM NO GOOD AT ALL, BUT HAD DEVELOPED INTO SOMETHING REALLY BAD FOR THESE TWO LYING SOULS.

EVIL SPIRIT'S DANCE

ONE FINE DAY, THIS GOOD-LOOKING SOUL WAS JUST LYING AROUND INSIDE HIS MUD HOUSE, JUST TAKING IT EASY RIGHT AFTER HE GOT HOME FROM BEING INVITED FOR DINNER, AND HE, OF COURSE, WAS FEELING NO PAIN, FOR HE WAS SOMEWHAT FULL AND, OF COURSE, SATISFIED BY HIS DAILY GIFT OF LIFE'S GOOD LUCK. SO AS FAR AS HE WAS CONCERNED, AS HE WAS MINDING HIS OWN BUSINESS AND NOT MUCH ELSE, AND WAS ABOUT TO DOZE OFF FOR HIS SOMEWHAT MUCH NEEDED DAILY NAP. HE HEARD SOMEONE CLIMB UP ONTO HIS MUD HOUSE SORT OF LOUDLY. THINKING THAT IT MAY BE ONE OF THE LITTLE CHILD SOULS FROM HIS HOME VILLAGE, WHOM HE DID ALWAYS HAVE VISITING HIM, HE WAS NOT TOO WORRIED ABOUT THAT SOMEONE DOING THE CLIMB TO THE TOP OF HIS MUD HOUSE. BUT WHEN THAT THING REACHED THE MIDDLE OF THE TOP OF HIS HOME, THE REALLY HANDSOME SOUL HEARD SOME MUSIC THAT WAS HEARD FOR THE VERY FIRST TIME BY THIS SAID GOOD-LOOKING SOUL. THEN, SOME DANCE MOVES WERE CARRIED OUT BY THAT THING UP ABOVE HIS MUD HOUSE, SO HE THEREFORE WENT

OUT TO DO SOME INVESTIGATING, TO FIND OUT WHAT THE COMMOTION WAS ALL ABOUT. WHAT HE DID SEE WHEN HE WAS OUTSIDE OF HIS MUD HOUSE REALLY SURPRISED HIM. IT WAS AN UGLY LITTLE EVIL SPIRIT, DOING SOME VERY STRANGE DANCE MOVES WITH HIMSELF, ALL ALONE, ON TOP OF HIS HOME. EVERY NOW AND THEN, THAT SMALL EVIL SPIRIT WOULD POINT ONE OF HIS LONG-NAILED FINGERS TOWARDS THE SEA, AND THE OT HER FINGER, ALSO EVILLY-NAILED, TOWARDS THIS GOOD-LOOKING LIVING SOUL. AND THEN, AFTER DOING SO, HE WOULD FALL ON HIS BACK, ALL THE WHILE HOLDING HIS STOMACH AREA, AND THEN HE WOULD START LAUGHING VERY UNCONTROLLABLY. AFTER OBSERVING THAT SMALL EVIL SPIRIT DOING WHAT HE HAD BEEN DOING AND REPEATING ALL OF WHAT THE SMALL EVIL SPIRIT WAS DOING, HE WENT BACK INSIDE HIS HOME TO DO HIS FAVORITE THING. THAT WAS TO LIE AROUND UNTIL MORNING, FOR HE WAS VERY WELL-LIKED ALL AROUND, AND HAD ALREADY BEEN INVITED FOR BREAKFAST BY SOMEONE. WHAT HE DID NOT KNOW HAPPENED SOMETIME EARLY THE NEXT MORNING. SOME ENEMY WARRIORS INVADED HIS SMALL HOME VILLAGE AND THEREFORE KILLED EVERY LIVING SOUL IN HIS SMALL HOME VILLAGE. AND WHENEVER THESE WARRIOR SOULS CAME TO HIS HOME, THEY JUST COULD NOT GET THEMSELVES TO POKE HIM WITH THEIR

SPEARS, AFTER SEEING THAT HE WAS VERY HANDSOME, INDEED, BUT BYPASSED HIM, KNOWING BEFOREHAND THAT ONLY ONE SOUL WAS TO BE LEFT ALIVE, SO THAT ONE LUCKY SOUL WOULD BE ALLOWED TO CARRY THE NEWS TO OTHER NEARBY VILLAGES THAT ALL HAD BEEN KILLED BY THE ENEMY, AND ALL THE FOOD HAD BEEN TAKEN. AFTERWARDS, THIS GOOD-LOOKING SOUL REALIZED WHAT THAT LITTLE EVIL DEMON KNEW, THAT ALL THOSE THAT HE LOVED VERY MUCH WOULD ALL DIE, AND THAT HE, THE HANDSOME SOUL, WOULD VERY MUCH BE SAVED BY HIS GOOD FACIAL FEATURES, AND BE CHOSEN AS A NEWS CARRIER OF SOMETHING THAT WAS VERY EVIL AND, NOT TO MENTION, REALLY BAD.

STEAM DOOR BLOCKED

THIS STEAMBATH-LOVING MAN SOUL ONE DAY WENT OUT TO THE WILDERNESS, IN HOPES OF FINDING SOME WOOD THAT THE OTHER SOULS, STILL BODILY ALIVE, IN HIS HOME VILLAGE MAY HAVE SOMEHOW MISSED OUT ON, OR HAD NOT BOTHERED TO PICK UP, DUE TO THEIR SOMEWHAT LAZY NATURES. HE HAD BEEN OUT IN THE WILDS FOR THE BETTER PART OF THAT DAY'S MORNING HOURS, DOING WHAT HE HAD IN HIS MIND THE PREVIOUS DAY, WHEN HE HAD GATHERED SOME WOOD. HE HAD TOLD HIMSELF THAT HE WOULD NOW BE ABLE TO TAKE HIS MUCH NEEDED SWEAT BATH. HE KNEW THAT ALL HIS BODY'S ACHES WOULD ALSO BE VERY MUCH RELIEVED AFTER SPENDING HIS EVENING HOURS DOING HIS SWEAT BATH ACTIVITY. WHEN HE GOT HOME, HE IMMEDIATELY CUT UP THE WOOD THAT HE, THE VERY MUCH BODILY ALIVE LIVING SOUL HAD GATHERED THAT MORNING. SOON AFTER HIS DINNER, HE LIT UP HIS FIRE. AND WHEN ALL WAS WARM, HOT, AND READY, HE TOOK HIS SO VERY NEEDED HOT STEAM. WHEN HE WAS RELAXED, VERY MUCH SO, INSIDE HIS SWEAT HOUSE, HE HAPPENED TO HEAR WHAT SEEMED LIKE A SINGLE KNOCK ON ONE OF

HIS SWEATHOUSE'S CORNERS. THINKING TO HIMSELF THAT NOISE WAS MADE BY THE EARTH'S COLD DIRT CRACKING, HE GAVE IT NO FURTHUR THOUGHT. AFTER SOME TIME, A SECOND KNOCK WAS HEARD BY THIS SWEAT-LOVING SOUL ON THE SECOND CORNER OF HIS STEAMHOUSE. THIS ONE WAS LOUDER THAN THE FIRST KNOCK. BUT HE DID NOT BOTHER TO CHECK IT OUT, FOR HE WAS NOT TOO CONCERNED ABOUT ANYTHING AT THAT MOMENT. LATER ON, HE DID HEAR THE THIRD CORNER KNOCK, VERY MUCH LOUDER THAN THE PREVIOUS TWO KNOCKS, AND DID THINK TO HIMSELF THAT HE WAS ALIVE ONLY ONCE IN HIS DAILY GIFT OF LIFE. BUT STILL, HE DID NOTHING BUT KEPT ON STEAMING. THEN, THE FOURTH AND FINAL KNOCK WAS EXTREMELY LOUD, AND THIS FINAL KNOCK SHOOK HIS STEAMHOUSE AND MISPLACED SOME HOT ROCKS ON HIS ONGOING BURNING FIRE. THIS GOT HIM SUDDENLY REALLY SCARED. BUT WHEN HE REACHED FOR THE STEAMHOUSE DOOR, HE COULD NOT FIND IT WHERE IT WAS SUPPOSED TO BE. WHEN PANIC SET IN HIS HEAD, HE STARTED TO DO SOME REALLY LOUD HOLLERING, AND POUNDED ON THE WOODEN WALLS OF HIS STEAMHOUSE. MUCH TO HIS DISMAY, HE STILL COULD NOT LOCATE THE DOORWAY SO THAT HE WOULD LIVE. AFTER ABOUT TEN MINUTES OF THIS HOLLERING THAT HE CARRIED OUT AT THE TOP OF HIS LUNGS, AND ALSO SOME HEAVY POUNDING

CARRIED OUT BY THIS POOR STEAMING, VERY MUCH STILL AMONG THE LIVING SOUL-WELL, WHAT TOOK PLACE WAS THIS: SOMEONE THAT HAPPENED TO BE PASSING HIS HOT STEAMHOUSE HEARD ALL THE COMMOTION COMING FROM THE STEAMHOUSE, AND DECIDED THAT HE WOULD CHECK OUT WHAT WAS GOING ON. HE FOUND OUT THAT ALL THOSE NOISES WERE COMING FROM THE INSIDE SECTION OF THIS STEAMHOUSE, AND OPENED THE DOOR FROM THE OUTSIDE. THIS, OF COURSE, DID SAVE THAT POOR SOUL THAT HAD PAID NO MIND TO THOSE STEAMHOUSE CORNER KNOCKS. THE POOR SOUL DID NOT EVEN BOTHER TO PUT HIS CLOTHES ON, BUT WENT BACK TO HIS HOUSE IMMEDIATELY. HE ALSO DID NOT BOTHER TO DRY OFF FIRST, FOR HE WAS AT HIS WIT'S END AT THAT VERY MOMENT IN TIME.

DEVIL'S BRIDE

ONE COLD EVENING, ALL THESE FUN-LOVING SOULS WERE INSIDE THE LOCALLY OWNED POOL HALL, DOING WHAT THEY HAPPENED TO HAVE A MIND TO CARRY OUT, AND THAT WAS TO PLAY SOME POOL WITH EACH OTHER. AND WHILE DOING SO, THEY WERE ALSO SNACKING OUT ON SOME OF THE EDIBLES THAT WERE ON THE GAME HALL'S FOOD MENU. THE EARLY EVENING HOURS WENT QUITE SMOOTHLY, WITH ALL OF THE ENTERTAINMENT AND FOOD GOING AS HAD BEEN EXPECTED. THAT PLEASED EVERYONE THAT HAPPENED TO BE PRESENT IN THAT GAME ROOM. WHAT DID HAPPEN AND OCCUR THAT FUN-FILLED DAY'S EVENING WAS THIS: A VERY BEAUTIFUL LADY DID HAPPEN TO STROLL INTO THAT BUILDING AT ABOUT FIFTEEN MINUTES BEFORE CLOSE DOWN. THIS VERY ADORABLE LADY IN QUESTION WAS WEARING CLOTHING THAT SEEMED TO BE STUDDED WITH PRECIOUS GEMS THAT WERE EXTREMELY BEAUTIFUL. THE DEAL WAS THIS: DESPITE THE COLD WEATHER AND ALL, SHE WAS NOT EVEN WEARING A COAT OR JACKET OF ANY SORT. WHEN SHE STARTED HER WALK FROM THE DOORWAY, THE WHOLE BUILDING OF SOULS

THAT HAD BEEN MAKING A BIG RACKET WERE SUDDENLY VERY QUIET, AND NO ONE WAS MAKING ANY NOISE WHATSOEVER. THAT WAS WHEN EVERYONE REALIZED THAT THIS VERY GOOD-LOOKING WOMAN HAD A TAIL ATTACHED TO HER, AND THAT WAS NOT A COMMON THING AMONG THOSE SOULS THAT WERE WITNESSING THIS VERY UNUSUAL APPEARANCE. THIS VERY CUTE GIRL DID HER STROLL WITH HER HEAD HELD HIGH AND A BIG SMILE ON HER VERY BEAUTIFUL FACE. WHEN SHE GOT TO AN EMPTY STOOL, SHE CAREFULLY SAT HERSELF DOWN AND DID NOT BOTHER TO LOOK AROUND, AS IF THE GAME-LOVING SOULS MEANT NOTHING TO HER. AND WHILE SHE SAT ON THAT STOOL, SHE SAT FACING THE WALL, SEEMING TO BE FULL OF PRIDE AND SOME UNKNOWN HAPPY, HAPPY THOUGHTS. ALL THE WHILE, SHE WAS STILL NOT LOOKING AROUND, AS IF SHE, THE VERY BEAUTIFUL AND FULL OF PRIDE AND HAPPINESS EVIL SPIRIT, WAS THE ONLY OCCUPANT OF THIS POOL ROOM. WHEN SOME TIME HAD PASSED AND THE USUALLY NOISY PLACE WAS STILL SHOCKINGLY QUIET (AND IT WAS VERY CLOSE TO THIS GAME ROOM'S CLOSING TIME) THE VERY BEAUTIFUL LADY, EVER COOL, AGAIN STOOD UP AND DID HER VERY LADYLIKE WALK TOWARDS THE DOOR, ALL THE WHILE STILL NOT LOOKING AROUND, BUT FULL OF SOMETHING THAT DID NOT BELONG IN THIS VERY GOOD WORLD OF OURS.

WHEN SHE GOT TO THE DOORWAY, SHE VERY DELICATELY OPENED IT UP, AND THEREFORE WENT OUT INTO THE VERY COLD NIGHT. AS SOON AS ALL HAD BEEN SAID AND DONE, SOMEONE WAS CURIOUS ENOUGH TO CHECK OUT WHERE THE VERY BEAUIFUL WOMAN WITH A LONG TAIL ATTACHED TO HER MAY BE HEADING OFF TO. BUT WHEN THIS VERY CURIOUS-MINDED SOUL WAS NOT INDOORS, SHE WAS NOWHERE TO BE SEEN. THERE WERE NO FOOTPRINTS ON THE FRESHLY FALLEN SNOW. AFTERWARDS, THE MANAGER CLOSED HIS POOL ROOM DOWN, LOCK, STOCK, AND BARREL, FOR HE WAS VERY AFRAID OF THE UNKNOWN AND THE UNUSUAL IN HIS SOMEWHAT RIGHT-FRAMED MIND.

DOG TALKED

THERE WAS A FAMINE THAT WAS MAKING ALL THE LIVES OF ALL THE VERY MUCH ALIVE AND BODILY-LIVING SOULS WHO HAPPENED TO BE IN THE THICK AND THEREFORE WERE EXPERIENCING THIS VERY, VERY BAD SITUATION, WHO WERE LIVING OUT THEIR DAILY GIFTS OF THEIR VERY VALUABLE LIVES. AND SO, THESE VERY ALIVE AND LIVING SOULS WERE IN A VERY BAD, BAD WAY. THIS ONE SOUL OF A MAN LIVED OUT IN THE WILDERNESS, AND THIS ONE MAN SOUL HAPPENED TO HAVE SOME DOGS THAT STILL HAD NOT BEEN KILLED OFF BY THIS FOOD SHORTAGE. AND ONE DAY, WHEN HE HAPPENED TO LOOK IN THE DIRECTION OF HIS HOME VILLAGE, HE SAW TWO STILL VERY ALIVE LIVING SOULS WHO WERE HEADING IN HIS MUD DWELLING'S DIRECTION. THESE TWO LIVING SOULS WERE FAST APPROCHING HIS PLACE OF EXISTENCE. THEY WERE WALKING, DUE TO THE FACT THAT ALL OF THE DOGS, OR MOST OF THEM, HAD ENDED UP IN THE COOKING POTS OF THESE VERY HUNGRY INDEED SOULS THAT STILL HAD NOT BEEN CLAIMED BY THE ONGOING SHORTAGE OF THINGS TO EAT AND THEREFORE, ENJOY.

WHEN THIS SOUL SAW THAT HE WAS ABOUT TO ENTERTAIN AND WOULD ALSO HAVE TO FEED THESE TWO LIVING SOULS HEADED HIS WAY, HE FOUND THAT THERE WAS NOT EVEN A SCRAP OF FOOD FOR HIM TO DO SOME COOKING WITH. HE KNEW THAT THESE TWO VERY MUCH ALIVE LIVING SOULS HEADED HIS WAY WOULD BE HUNGRY, AND ALSO KNEW THAT THEY WOULD BE VERY MALNOURISHED, DUE TO ALL THE GOOD THINGS TO EAT NOT BEING THERE FOR EVERY LIVING SOUL TO ENJOY, BECAUSE OF THE CONTINUED FAMINE, WHICH WAS STILL GOING FAST FORWARD THROUGHOUT THE LAND, WHERE THESE BODILY ALIVE, YET NOT-SO-WELL-OFF LIVING SOULS WERE. SO THIS MAN IN QUESTION DECIDED IN HIS YET STILL VERY CONSCIOUS HEAD THAT HE BY HIS OWN FREE WILL AND POWER WOULD THEREFORE GO AND KILL OFF ONE OF HIS REMAINING DOGS TO FEED THESE ONCOMING SOULS THAT WERE HEADED HIS WAY. WHEN THIS SOUL GOT AROUND TO THE AREA WHERE HE KEPT HIS DOGS TIED UP, HOLDING A BIG PIECE OF STICK THAT HE COULD USE TO KILL ONE OF THEM FOR HIS ONCOMING GUESTS, HE HAPPENED TO LOOK THEM OVER. HE SAW HIS VERY OLD DOG TEAM LEADER AND DECIDED THAT THEY WOULD LOOK HIM UP AND HAVE HIM FOR DINNER. WHEN HE HEADED TOWARDS HIM, THE OLD DOG IN QUESTION SEEMED TO KNOW HIS COMING FATE, AND WAS VERY DOWNCAST. HE SEEMED VERY SAD.

AS SOON AS THIS HUNGRY SOUL GOT TO HIM AND WAS ABOUT TO CLUB HIM TO DEATH, THE OLD DOG SUDDENLY LOOKED UP AT HIM WITH SADNESS IN HIS EYES, AND ASKED HIM THIS: "HOW MANY TIMES HAVE I SAVED YOUR LIFE?" THAT DOG TALKING SHOOK UP THIS SOUL, AND HE DID REMEMBER THAT YES, THIS OLD DOG DID SAVE HIS LIFE MORE THAN HE COULD COUNT. SO HE THEREFORE DID NOT KILL THAT OLD DOG, BUT CHOSE ANOTHER DOG THAT HE COULD KILL, BUTCHER, AND HAVE FOR DINNER FOR HIMSELF AND THOSE TWO OTHER SOULS WHO WERE VERY HUNGRY, INDEED, DUE TO THAT HEARTLESS AND VERY MERCILESS ONGOING FAMINE OF THE LAND THAT THEY KNEW WOULD END VERY SOON.

HELPFUL LITTLE IMP

A VERY OLD LIVING SOUL ONE DAY MADE UP HER MIND THAT SHE WOULD BE OUT GATHERING SMALL PIECES OF TREE BRANCHES THAT SHE, THE VERY OLD SOUL, WOULD USE, THEREFORE, TO COOK HER FOOD WITH. FOR SHE HAD USED UP HER LAST MERGER OF TWIGS THAT SHE HAD PREVIOUSLY GATHERED FOR HER COOKING PURPOSES, WHICH SHE STILL DID ON A DAILY BASIS, FROM SOME OF THE RAW MEAT FROM HER FELLOW VILLAGER SOULS THAT HAPPENED TO BE AT HER MUD HOUSE DWELLING PLACE ON A SOMEWHAT REGULAR BASIS. THEY KNEW BEFOREHAND THAT THIS VERY OLD SOUL IN QUESTION DID NOT HAVE ANY SONS AND THAT HER FORMER HUSBAND HAD DIED BODILY A LONG WHILE BACK. SHE DID PREPARE FOR HERSELF SOME DRIED MEAT THAT SHE COULD CONSUME ON HER TWIG-GATHERING DAY, KNOWING IN HER STILL VERY SANE MIND THAT SHE WOULD BE HUNGRY SOMETIME DURING THE COURSE OF THAT DAY ON HER TWIG MISSION. THEREFORE, WHEN ALL WAS READY, SHE STARTED HER CHORE OF WALKING OUT TO THE BEACH AREA QUITE SLOWLY, FOR SHE WAS NO LONGER HER FORMERLY FULL-OF-ENERGY SELF, BUT

WAS PREOCCUPIED BY THE DAILY ACHES AND BODY PAINS THAT WERE ASSOCIATED WITH ADVANCED LONG LIFE. WHEN SHE DID FINALLY REACH THE BEACH AREA, SHE DID SOME TWIG GATHERING, STOPPING TO REST UP MORE THAN SHE HAD HOPED TO DO. AT ABOUT THE TIME FOR HER LUNCH BREAK, SHE SPOTTED A BEACHY, GRASSED-UP AREA THAT SHE THEREFORE SAT ON AND DID NOT EAT UP RIGHT AWAY, BUT SAT AROUND FOR A LONG WHILE WITH HER EYES FULLY CLOSED. WHEN SHE HAPPENED TO HEAR SOMETHING THAT SEEMED TO BE OF AN UNCOMFORTABLE SITUATION, SHE OPENED HER EYES TO SEE WHAT WAS MAKING THAT CRY-LIKE NOISE. WHAT SHE SAW IN FRONT OF HER WAS AN UGLY LITTLE DEVIL IMP, WHOSE OTHER EYE WAS BLOODSHOT RED, AND SEEMED TO BE IN A VERY BAD WAY. THAT VERY EVIL LITTLE DEMON THEN TOLD HER IN HIS EVIL-SOUNDING VOICE THAT SOMETHING WAS IN HIS BLOODSHOT EYE, AND THAT HE COULD NOT REMOVE IT HIMSELF, DESPITE HIS ONGOING EFFORTS TO DO SO. HE ASKED HER IF SHE WOULD HAVE THE GOODNESS WITHIN HER HEART TO HELP HIM OUT OF HIS BIT PROBLEM, WHICH WAS THAT SOMETHING WAS STUCK IN ONE OF HIS EYES. THE OLD SOUL DID FEEL SORRY FOR THAT UGLY LITTLE DEMON, AND TOLD HIM THAT SHE WOULD HELP HIM OUT THE BEST SHE KNEW HOW. WHEN THE OLD SOUL HAD A LOOK IN HIS BLOODSHOT EYE, SHE FOUND

OUT THAT THE PROBLEM HAD BEEN A PIECE OF HAIR, LODGED DEEPLY INSIDE THIS EVIL LITTLE DEMON'S EYE. SHE REMOVED THAT PIECE OF HAIR FROM THAT LITTLE IMP'S EYE. THEN, THE LITTLE EVIL THING TOLD HER THAT A BIG SURPRISE AWAITED HER, AND DISAPPEARED FROM HER SIGHT. AFTERWARDS, THIS OLD SOUL THEN WENT HOME WITH HER SMALL TWIGS THAT SHE HAD GATHERED THAT DAY. WHEN SHE WOKE UP THE NEXT MORNING, SHE FOUND A YEAR'S SUPPLY OF DRY WOOD JUST OUTSIDE OF HER MUD DWELLING, AND WAS VERY GRATFUL, AND THANKED THAT LITTLE UGLY EVIL DEMON, IN HER MIND AND ALSO VERBALLY, FOR ALL THE WOOD THAT HE HAD SOMEHOW GATHERED FOR HER SOMETIME DURING THE NIGHT.

UNBELIEVERS' COMING DESTINATION

THIS VERY EVIL-MINDED, VERY ALIVE, BODILY LIVING SOUL LIVED IN THIS ONE SMALL VILLAGE. AND WHAT WAS SO EVIL ABOUT THIS EVIL, EVIL SOUL BOY? WELL, IT HAPPENED TO START UP ABOUT TEN OR MORE YEARS AGO IN HIS EVIL DAYS PAST, WHILE HE WAS UNKNOWINGLY USING HIS DAILY GIFT OF HIS PRECIOUS LIFE JUST TO DO BAD THINGS, SO THAT THOSE OTHER POOR SOULS WOULD HAVE BAD DAYS, OR WOULD HAVE THEIR SOMEWHAT GOOD DAYS RUINED AND TURNED INTO BAD DAYS BY THE ONGOING DEEDS OF THIS BAD SOUL DOING GREAT EVIL. THIS EVIL SOUL BOY WOULD OFTEN GO AROUND HIS HOME VILLAGE AND PROVOKE THOSE OTHER POOR SOULS INTO BEING ANGRY WITH HIM, AND THIS EVIL-MINDED BOY WOULD VERY OFTEN WIN ALL THE ARGUMENTS AND WHATNOT, FOR HE WAS A VERY SMOOTH-TALKING BAD SOUL, AND ALSO KNEW WHAT KIND OF TALK WOULD THEREFORE MAKE THE OTHER LIVING SOULS HAVE BAD DAYS. DAY IN AND DAY OUT, HE SOMETIMES WOULD GET THREATENED BY SOME OF THE BIG SOULS, BUT WOULD TELL THEM THAT IF THEY DID NOT CARRY OUT THEIR THREATS, THE EVIL SOUL BOY WOULD PUT

THEM IN THE HOSPITAL, AND THAT ALWAYS
WOULD MAKE THE BIG SOULS BACK OFF, FOR
THEY ALREADY KNEW THAT HIS MIND SEEMED
NOT TO BE WORKING TOO WELL. HIS NIGHTLY
DREAMS CONSISTED OF HIM GETTING INTO
FIGHTS WITH VERY FOUL-ODORED DEMONS.
THE DEMONS IN HIS DREAMS WERE VERY
STRONG, UNBEATABLE, AND VERY SCARY,
ALSO. WHENEVER HE DREAMED ABOUT THE
DEVIL, THE MOST EVIL OF THEM ALL, THE
DEVIL WOULD LOOK REALLY HANDSOME,
WITH YELLOW HAIR AND SNAKE-LIKE EYES,
AND WOULD OFTEN POINT OUT TO THIS EVIL-
MINDED SOUL THE POINTS THAT HE, THE
DEVIL, WAS MUCH BETTER ON THAN GOD. AND
SOMETIMES, HE WOULD LET THIS EVIL SOUL
BOY RUN HIS FINGERS THROUGH HIS GOLDEN
HAIR, AND TELL HIM HOW GOOD HE WAS. HE
WOULD OFTEN THANK THE EVIL SOUL FOR
SERVING HIM ONLY. SO, THIS EVIL SOUL HAD A
SOMEWHAT DIFFERENT OPINION OF THE MOST
EVIL OF ALL LIVING SUPERNATURAL SPIRITS
AROUND AND ABOUT TO THIS VERY DAY. WELL
THEN, ALL WOULD ONE DAY COME OUT ABOUT
WHAT WAS WHAT, AND HOW WRONG THIS
EVIL SOUL BOY HAD BEEN ALL ALONG ABOUT
THE DEVIL AND HIS VERY EVIL DEMONS. ONE
NIGHT, HE HAD A VERY DIFFERENT DREAM
THAT HIS DAILY GIFT OF LIFE HAD ENDED AND
WAS TAKEN BY THOSE VERY FOUL-ODORED
DEMONS BELOW THE EARTH. HE SAW LOST
SOULS THERE, CRYING AND BEING TORTURED

BY DEMONS, BY USE OF VERY, VERY HOT FIRES, AND VERY GREAT TORMENTS. WHEN HE WAS BROUGHT BEFORE THE DEVIL, THE MOST EVIL OF ALL DID JUDGE HIM AFTER A DIRTY BOOK WAS BROUGHT TO HIM. HE DISHED OUT THIS POOR EVIL SOUL'S COMING PUNISHMENT FOR HIS BAD DEEDS, WHICH HE HAD DONE WHILE HE WAS YET STILL ALIVE AND WELL ON EARTH. WHEN ALL WAS SAID AND DONE, THE VERY STRONG AND FOUL-SMELLING DEMONS BROUGHT THE EVIL BOY TO A SMALL BOX-LIKE OBJECT AND STUFFED HIM INSIDE THIS SMALL METAL THING WITH HIS LEGS BENDED, DESPITE HIS STRUGGLES TO GET FREE. THEY CLOSED THE SMALL METAL DOOR OF THIS METAL STOVE. THE POOR EVIL SOUL WAS OVERCOME BY THE DARKNESS INSIDE, AND WHEN THE DEMONS TURNED ON THE FIRE THAT WAS VERY, VERY HOT, THIS POOR EVIL BOY WOKE UP SCREAMING AND CRYING AT THE SAME TIME, AFTER BEING INSIDE THAT VERY HOT FIRE FOR ABOUT THREE SECONDS OR SO. AFTERWARDS, THIS VERY EVIL SOUL CHANGED HIS WAYS, AFTER SEEING WHAT REALLY HAPPENS AFTER A PERSON HAS DIED BODILY. HE ALSO FOUND OUT THAT THE SOUL DOES NOT DIE, BUT IS TRANSPORTED EITHER TO HEAVEN OR TO HELL, WHICH IS BELOW THE EARTH, TO BE TORTURED BY DEMONS, BY THE USE OF VERY, VERY HOT FIRES AND OTHER UNDREAMED-OF METHODS, AS THEY ARE ORDERED TO DO BY THE MOST EVIL OF

ALL SUPERNATURAL SPIRITS. HE IS MORE OFTEN THOUGHT OF AS BEING NOT SO BAD, BUT IS MORE EVIL THAN WHAT PEOPLE MAY THINK. THE DEVIL, OR ENEMY OF ALL HUMAN RACES, HATES VERY, VERY MUCH, AND DOES WANT EVERY LIVING SOUL, SO HE COULD TORTURE AND TORMENT THEM BY THE USE OF VERY HOT FIRES AFTER THEY HAVE DIED BODILY.

KILLER MUKLUKS

THIS ONE LIVING SOUL, WHO STOLE STUFF, HAPPENED TO LIVE AND EXIST IN THIS ONE SMALL VILLAGE, AND STOLE OTHERS' WORLDLY POSSESSIONS ON A SOMEWHAT DAILY BASIS. THIS SOUL DID THEREFORE MAKE SOME OF THE VERY MUCH ALIVE SOULS, LIVING OUT THEIR ONGOING PRECIOUS DAILY GIFTS OF THEIR LIVES. VERY MUCH SO. NOT SO YES. FOR THIS SOUL IN QUESTION WOULD STEAL ANYTHING THAT HE COULD GET HIS HANDS ON, USE IT ONLY ONCE, AND LEAVE IT SOMEWHERE ELSE AFTER HE NO LONGER NEEDED TO USE IT FOR HIS SOMEWHAT ONGOING NEED TO USE IT AND LEAVE IT ON A DAILY BASIS. HE WOULD SEEM ALWAYS TO BE IN NO NEED OF ANYTHING USEFUL, BUT DID ALWAYS HAVE STUFF AT HIS DISPOSAL, DUE TO HIS VERY BUSY HANDS THAT HE USED TO DO THESE BAD, BAD THINGS. THEY WERE BAD IN THE EYES OF HIS FELLOW VILLAGER SOULS, AND WERE NOT APPRECIATED ONE BIT BY OTHERS THAT WERE CONSTANTLY LOSING STUFF TO THIS MAN SOUL WHO DID NOT MAKE STUFF, AS FAR AS THE WHOLE VILLAGE AS UNIT COULD SEE. BUT HE WOULD ONE DAY SEE THAT TAKING SOME STUFF DOES INDEED

HAVE A VERY BAD ENGING. THESE OTHER VICTIMS OF THIS LIVING SOUL MADE PLANS THAT THEY WOULD HANG THESE SOMEWHAT NEW MUKLUKS THAT HAD BEEN OWNED BY A NEWLY DEARLY DEPARTED FORMER LOVED ONE, WHO HAD JUST BODILY DIED. AND THEY HUNG THOSE MUKLUKS ON A SPOT THAT WAS HARD FOR THIS SOUL, WHO ALWAYS HAD THEFT ON HIS MIND, TO MISS. AND SURE ENOUGH, THOSE MUKLUKS TURNED UP MISSING THAT VERY SAME DAY THAT THEY WERE HUNG UP ON PURPOSE TO TEACH THIS THIEVING SOUL A LESSON. THAT VERY SAME NIGHT, THIS BAD SOUL, WHO TOOK THEM AND RAN, FELT SOMETHING WALKING ON HIS BODY WHILE HE WAS ASLEEP. AND PRETTY SOON, THOSE FEET STARTED KICKING HIM ON HIS FACE. THINKING THAT SOMEONE WAS TRYING TO END HIS GIFT OF DAILY LIFE, THIS ROBBING SOUL GOT UP SWINGING HIS FISTS QUITE QUICKLY. BUT THEN HE REALIZED THAT HE WASN'T HITTING ANYTHING SOLID, BUT WAS PUNCHING OUT INTO THIN AIR, HITTING OR GETTING NOWHERE WITH WHAT HE WAS CARRYING OUT AT THAT VERY MOMENT. THEN, WHEN HE FINALLY REALIZED THAT HE WAS STILL AT GROUND ZERO, HE SAW THEM COMING AT HIM. AND WHAT HE SAW WERE THOSE MUKLUKS, WITHOUT A BODY THAT THEY COULD EVEN SAY WAS THEIR OWNER. BUT THEY WERE ALL ALONE, THE PAIR OF THOSE MUKLUKS, THAT HAD PLANNED ON

USING THAT VERY DAY'S MORNING TIME. THIS VERY WEIRD OCCURRENCE SCARED THAT POOR LIVING SOUL OUT OF HIS WITS. SO HE RAN OUT OF HIS MUD DWELLING PLACE AND THEREFORE SPENT HIS NIGHT OUT IN HIS MUD SWEATHOUSE. EARLY THE NEXT MORNING, THIS NEVER-ASK-FIRST LIVING SOUL BURNED DOWN HIS HUT, USING SEAL OIL TO DO THE JOB. AND HE DID NOT FIRST GO INSIDE TO RETRIEVE ALL THE STOLEN GOODIES THAT HE HAD ALREADY TAKEN, FOR HE WAS STILL SCARED STIFF. AFTERWARDS, HE STOPPED HIS STEALING WAYS, AND RATHER, MADE SOME USEFUL STUFF THAT HE COULD GIVE AWAY AS GIFTS TO THE LIVING SOULS THAT WERE STILL ALIVE AND WELL BACK IN HIS HOME VILLAGE.

SELF EATER

THERE LIVED A MAN AND HIS VERY MUCH LOVED WIFE. THESE TWO LIVING AND VERY MUCH ALIVE SOULS HAPPENED TO CARRY OUT THEIR DAILY GIFTS OF THEIR LIVES IN THE WILDERNESS, AWAY FROM THE OTHER LIVING SOULS THAT WERE DOING THE SAME BACK IN THEIR HOME VILLAGE. AND WHAT THESE VERY POOR SOULS WERE EXPERIENCING AT THAT TIME WAS THE ONGOING, RELENTLESS, AND VERY MERCILESS SHORTAGE OF GOOD THINGS THAT THEY THEREFORE COULD CONSUME--IN OTHER WORDS, EAT. FOR THERE WAS A FAMINE IN THE IMMEDIATE AREA, IN WHICH THESE TWO WERE LIVING OUT THEIR ONGOING DAILY GIFTS OF THEIR SOMEWHAT VERY HARD-TO-SWALLOW LIVES, DUE TO THAT NOTHING TO EAT THING GOING ON AT THAT VERY MOMENT IN TIME. AND EVERY SOUL ALIVE DID HAVE A HARD TIME OF FINDING ANYTHING TO EAT. ONE DAY, THE MAN SOUL SAID TO HIS MUCH LOVED WIFE THAT HE WAS GOING DOWN TO THE RIVER TO TRY HIS LUCK AT CATCHING SOMETHING FROM THE WATER--IN THIS CASE, A FISH, OR MAYBE TWO. THE WIFE THEN TOLD HIM TO BE CAREFUL, AND TOLD HIM TO BE SAFE, ALSO. SO THE MAN

SOULTOOK OFF TO THE RIVER TO DO SOME FISHING IN HOPES OF CATCHING A FISH THAT HE AND HIS WIFE COULD THEREFORE EAT AND STRENGTHEN THEMSELVES WITH. THE SOUL MAN WAS GONE FROM HIS HOME ALL MORNING. WHEN THE AFTERNOON HOURS ROLLED AROUND, THE WIFE WAS GETTING VERY WORRIED FOR THE SAFTY OF HER MAN. SO, SHE GOT HERSELF READIED UP, SO THAT SHE COULD CHECK ON HIM AND SEE FOR HERSELF HOW HE WAS DOING ON HIS FISH-GETTING MISSION. WHEN SHE REACHED THE RIVER AREA, SHE DID SEE HER MAN SITTING ON TOP OF THE ICE, AND WHAT MADE HER MOVE, NEARLY RUNNING, WAS THIS: HER MAN HADN'T MOVED EVEN ONCE FROM THE TIME THAT SHE HAD SPOTTED HIM FROM QUITE A DISTANCE AWAY. AND WHEN SHE FINALLY REACHED HIM, HER WORST FEARS WERE ANSWERED, RIGHT THERE ON THE SPOT, FOR SHE FOUND HER MAN WAS NOW BODILY DEAD, AND THERE WAS QUITE A VOLUME OF SPILLED BLOOD SURROUNDING HER FORMER HUSBAND, WHO WAS NOW REALLY DEAD, AS FAR AS THINGS WENT. SHE SAW THAT HE HAD TRIED HIS HAND AT FISHING FOR FOOD, FOR THERE WAS A FISHING HOLE THAT HAD BEEN CHOPPED THROUGH THE ICE. SHE SAW HIS FISHING EQUIPMENT NEAR HIS NOW DEAD BODY, BUT SAW FOR HERSELF THAT HE HAD NOT HAD ANY LUCK CATCHING ANY FISH, BUT THAT HER FORMER HUSBAND HAD

DONE A VERY BAD THING, INDEED. THE POOR SOUL HAD CUT OUT A BIG PIECE OF HIS LEG'S SECTION AND HAD EATEN SOME OF HIS OWN LEG AFTER HE HAD CHOPPED SOME FLESH OFF HIMSELF. BUT HE HAD BLED TO DEATH FROM HIS WOUND, WHICH HE HAD DONE TO HIMSELF AFTER TRYING TO CATCH SOME FISH THROUGH THAT RIVER ICE, WHERE NO FISH WERE EVEN CAUGHT ON THAT VERY BAD DAY, WHICH THE POOR SOUL WAS VERY MUCH HOPING FOR. BUT HE HAD TRIED TO EAT HIMSELF, WHICH LED TO HIMSELF BEING NO LONGER ALIVE BODILY. BUT HE WAS STILL ALIVE IN SPIRIT, SOMEWHERE, EITHER IN A VERY BEAUTIFUL PLACE, OR IN A VERY BAD PLACE, ALSO IN SPIRIT.

DEVIL'S WARNING VISIT

THERE DID HAPPEN TO BE A WOMAN WITH
A SOUL WHO LOVED CARD PLAYING AND WAS
VERY BODILY ALIVE. THIS WOMAN SOUL'S
DAY-IN AND DAY-OUT ACTIVITY, ACCORDING
TO HER WISHES, WAS TO PLAY FOR MONEY
WITH ALL THE OTHER CARD SOULS THAT SHE
HAPPENED TO CARRY OUT HER MUCH LOVED
THING WITH. AND ALL OF HER DAY-IN AND DAY-
OUT DAILY THOUGHTS WERE CONCENTRATED
ON ONLY ONE THING, AND THAT WAS TO DO
SOME WINNING WITH HER VERY OWN CARD-
PLAYING SKILLS THAT SHE AND THE OTHER
SOULS KNEW. SHE, THE CARDS WOMAN
SOUL, WAS A VERY SHARP PLAYER AND
DID NOT OFTEN LOSE, FOR AFTER SHE HAD
WON SOME MONEY, WHICH SHE OFTEN DID
ON A REGULAR BASIS, SHE HAD A HABIT OF
QUITTING WHENEVER HER LUCK WAS USED
UP, SO TO SAY, SO THEN SHE WOULD HAVE
FUNDS FOR HER HABIT THE VERY NEXT DAY.
FOR HER TO BE IN THE CARD GAMES WAS
INDEED A VERY TRUE FACT. BUT ONE OF THOSE
NIGHTS THAT SEEMED TO BE ON HER WINNING
SIDE WERE SOMEWHAT MISSING, AS SHE HAD
WISHED NOT FOR IT TO EVER HAPPEN TO HER.
ON THIS NIGHT IN QUESTION, ALL HER LUCK

WAS GONE AND SHE ALSO HAD TO BORROW SOME MONEY FROM ALL THE OTHER CARD SOULS. THAT NIGHT, WHICH WAS VERY BAD FOR HER ALONE, WHEN SHE WAS IN DEBT, SHE DECIDED THAT SHE WOULD HEAD ON HOME AND SLEEP OFF HER VERY BAD NIGHT. WHEN SHE GOT TO HER HOUSE, SHE MADE SURE THAT HER PORCH DOOR WAS LOCKED. THIS WOMAN SOUL ALSO LOCKED UP THE DOOR LEADING TO HER MAIN HOUSE WHILE SHE WAS HAVING HER CUP OF TEA. SHE WAS THINKING ABOUT THAT CARD GAME, STILL GOING ON AT HER BEST FRIEND'S HOUSE. AFTER HER SNACK BEFORE BED, SHE WENT TO BED. AS SOON AS SHE HAD TURNED HER LIGHT OFF AND LAY ON HER PILLOW, SHE HEARD HER PORCH DOOR OPEN UP, AND ALSO HEARD SOME FOOTSTEPS; THEN, THE INNER DOOR OF HER HOUSE OPENED UP AND SOMEONE CAME INTO HER HOUSE. SHE WAS NOW VERY SCARED, KNOWING THAT SHE HAD LOCKED UP BOTH THE INSIDE AND OUTSIDE DOORS. THEN, THAT SOMEONE TOLD HER THAT HE WAS THE DEVIL, AND SAID TO HER THAT IF HE WANTED TO HAVE HER SOUL AT THAT VERY MOMENT, HE COULD TAKE IT. AND AS SOON AS HE, THE MOST EVIL OF ALL, HAD SAID THIS TO HER, THE CARD-LOVING, LIVING SOUL, SHE STARTED PRAYING VERY TRULY IN HER HEART. AND AS SOON AS THE EVIL DEVIL HEARD HER PRAYING, HE TOLD HER TO KEEP ON SERVING HIM ALONE AND

PROMISED HER THAT HE WOULD GIVE HER
WHATEVER SHE WANTED, AND ALSO, THAT
A VERY LONG LIFE WAS IN STORE FOR HER.
AND AS SOON AS SHE HAD SAID HER AMEN,
THE EVIL THING DID LEAVE HER PLACE, AGAIN
OPENING THE FRONT DOOR, AND FOOTSTEPS
COULD ALSO BE HEARD LEAVING HER PLACE.
AFTER HE, THE MOST EVIL ONE OF ALL, HAD
LEFT HER PLACE, SHE, THE WOMAN SOUL,
GOT HERSELF UP TO CHECK ON HER DOORS.
AND SURE ENOUGH, ALL OF HER DOORS
WERE ALL LOCKED UP. AFTER THIS VERY BAD
INCIDENT, THE CARD-LOVING SOUL CHANGED
HER WAYS AND STOPPED HER CARD PLAYING
ALTOGETHER. SHE STARTED GOING TO
CHURCH ON A VERY REGULAR BASIS, AFTER
GETTING TO KNOW THAT THE MOST EVIL ONE
WAS OUT TO DESTROY HER BODY, AND CLAIM
HER SOUL FOR HIMSELF SO THAT HE COULD
DO WHATEVER HE WANTED TO DO WITH IT
AFTER HER BODY HAD DIED OFF.

BIRDS RETURN UNBELIEVER

THERE LIVED A LIVING SOUL, WHICH, IN THIS CASE, WAS A MAN. THIS SOUL IN QUESTION WAS INDEED ONE OF THOSE HOT-HEADED TYPES OF SOUL MEN, AND THIS MAN IN QUESTION LIVED IN THIS VERY SMALL VILLAGE THAT CONSISTED OF LESS THAN A HUNDRED SOULS ALTOGETHER, WHO WERE CARRYING OUT THEIR DAILY GIFTS OF THEIR LIVES. THEY HAPPENED TO BE LIVING OUT THEIR DAILY EXISTENCES IN OUR VERY GOOD HOME, THE EARTH, IN THAT SOMEWHAT SMALL VILLAGE. AND THIS NOT-SO-RIGHT-IN-HIS-HEAD SOUL OF MAN WOULD OFTEN GO AROUND IN THIS SMALL VILLAGE AND VOICE HIS OPINIONS ABOUT THE SPIRIT WORLD. HE WOULD SAY THAT ANY OLD EVIL SPIRIT COULD THEREFORE BE BEATEN BY HIM, AND ALSO, HE STATED THAT HE WAS SCARED OF NOTHING. AT THE TIME WHEN THE BIRDS RETURN FROM THEIR WINTER GETAWAY--IN THIS CASE, IT WAS SPRINGTIME--THIS POOR SOUL, WHO NEVER LISTENED OR DID AS HE HAD BEEN TOLD, VERY ALIVE SOUL MADE HIS ROUNDS VISITING THE OTHER LIVING SOULS' HOMES. HE WOULD GO TO BED THAT SAME EVENING WITHOUT COVERING UP HIS WINDOW. ALSO,

HE DID SOME BIG TALK TO WHOMEVER HE MET, OUT IN HIS SMALL HOME VILLAGE THAT VERY SAME DAY, ABOUT HIS UPCOMING INTENTIONS FOR THAT NIGHT. THAT WAS THAT HE WAS IN HIS RIGHT FRAME OF MIND, AND THAT NO OLD BIRD RETURNING FROM THE SOUTH WAS ABOUT TO DO HIM ANY HARM. ALL THOSE THAT THIS SOUL IN QUESTION HAD HIS TALKS WITH TRIED TO CAUTION HIM AND TALK HIM OUT OF HIS SELF-CENTERED NATURE. ALSO, SOME TOLD HIM THAT THIS SORT OF VERY WRONG THING TO DO HAD BEEN CAUTIONED AGAINST TO ALL THE VERY ALIVE SOULS FROM A LONG TIME AGO PAST, AND WAS STILL TOLD TO ALL SOULS ALIVE, SO THAT NO HARM MAY BEFALL THEM WHENEVER THE SPRINGTIME CAME AROUND. BUT FOR THIS SOUL MAN, WHO HAD HAD HIS FILL OF THE MANY THINGS THAT ALL ALIVE SOULS WERE STILL TOLD NOT TO DO, WOULD SEE BY HIMSELF THAT YES, THE EVIL SPIRITS WERE VERY CAPABLE OF DESTROYING ONE'S BODY. THAT UNLUCKY MAN DID WHAT HE HAD INTENDED TO CARRY OUT THAT SAME NIGHT, AND THAT WAS TO GO TO BED WITHOUT COVERING UP HIS WINDOW. THE NEXT DAY, WHEN THIS SOUL THAT WOULD NOT LISTEN UP HAD NOT BEEN SEEN DOING HIS USUAL WALKS AROUND HIS HOME VILLAGE, AND ALSO HAD NOT DONE HIS VISITS TO SOME OF HIS FELLOW VILLAGER SOULS' PLACES, SOMEONE GOT CONCERNED FOR HIS SAFETY AND WELL-BEING. FOR

THIS SOUL IN QUESTION HAD STATED THE PRECEDING DAY THAT HE WOULD GO OFF TO SLEEP WITHOUT COVERING UP HIS WINDOW. WHEN THIS VERY ALIVE SOUL GOT TO THAT MAN'S HOUSE, HE SAW HIM ON HIS BED STILL, BUT UPON CLOSER VIEWING, HE SAW THAT HE HAD DIED BODILY SOMETIME DURING THE NIGHT. BUT THE THING WAS, THIS DEAD MAN'S EYES WERE STILL VERY OPEN. ONE OF HIS EYES WAS LOOKING AT THAT OPEN WINDOW, AND HIS OTHER EYE WAS LOOKING AT HIS DOORWAY. AFTER SEEING ALL,.T HE CONCERNED SOUL SAW THAT HE, THE NOW BODILY DEAD MAN, HAD CARRIED OUT WHAT HE HAD INTENTED TO DO, BUT IT HAD COST HIM HIS LIFE, BECAUSE HE DID NOT BELIEVE IN EVIL SPIRITS WHO WERE OUT TO HARM ALL WHENEVER THE BIRDS RETURNED EVERY SPRING. AND HE DID PROVE TO EVERY SOUL ALIVE THAT THE WARNINGS WERE QUITE TRUE FOR THOSE WARNINGS.

GOOD SOUL'S REWARD

THIS VERY YOUNG SOUL, WHO HAPPENED TO LIVE IN THIS VERY SMALL VILLAGE, WAS A VERY HELPFUL, GOOD SOUL. HE DID ALL THAT WAS BEING CARRIED OUT BY HIMSELF AT THAT TIME, WHICH WAS FOR HIM AND HIM ALONE TO LIVE OUT, DOING ALL THAT HE HIMSELF HAD THEREFORE BEEN BORN TO DO. THAT WAS TO HELP OUT ALL THE VILLAGE SOULS WITH THE DAILY CHORES THAT NEEDED TO BE TAKEN CARE OF ON A DAILY BASIS. AND THIS VERY GOOD-HEARTED LIVING SOUL DID DO A LOT OF GOOD THINGS FOR HIS FELLOW MEN. THE VERY GOOD-HEARTED LIVING SOUL WOULD MAKE SURE THAT THE VILLAGE'S AREA WAS SOMEWHAT CLEAN OF FOOD OR ANIMAL LEFTOVERS, AND MADE SURE THAT THE ICE HOLD THAT WAS USED BY HIS FELLOW VILLAGE SOULS TO FETCH THEIR DAILY WATER DID NOT FREEZE OVER, BY OPENING IT UP USING SOMETHING RESEMBLING AN ICE PICK. EACH AND EVERY MORNING, HE ALSO WENT TO EACH AND EVERY HOUSE TO DUMP THESE OTHER LIVING SOULS' WASTE CONTAINER BUCKETS FOR THEM. WELL, THIS VERY GOOD-HEARTED, VERY MUCH BODILY ALIVE LIVING SOUL DID THIS SORT OF GOOD

THING, HELPING OUT HIS FELLOW VILLAGER SOULS SINCE SOME TIME BACK IN HIS VERY GOOD-HEARTED PAST. IT WAS LIKELY MORE THAN TEN YEARS OR SO AGO, AND HE DID NOT BACK DOWN OR GIVE UP HIS GOODNESS, FOR HE WAS NOT THE LAZY SORT THAT MOST OF US ARE VERY MUCH INTO THESE DAYS. BUT HE DID ALL OF THE ABOVE, DAY IN AND DAY OUT, EVERY SINGLE DAY. HE HELPED EACH AND EVERY SOUL THAT HE CAME IN CONTACT WITH EVERY DAY, AND ALL OF THE VILLAGE'S LIVING SOULS ASKED HIM FOR HIS HELP WHENEVER THEY HAPPENED TO BE DOING SOMETHING THAT REQUIRED THE STRENGTH OF TWO MEN TO FINISH THE JOB, FOR THEY ALREADY KNEW THAT HE WOULD NOT TALK BACK OR LIE TO THEM. THEY KNEW THAT HE WAS TOO BUSY AT THAT MOMENT TO LEND HIS HELPING HANDS, SO HE WAS IN FACT HELPING OUT THOSE IN NEED OF HIS VERY MUCH APPRECIATED HELP ON A SOMEWHAT DAILY BASIS. BUT QUITE SOON, THE OTHER VILLAGERS WOULD SEE THIS GOOD-HEARTED LIVING SOUL WHILE HE WAS OUT AND ABOUT, AND WHAT THESE OTHER SOULS SAW WAS THIS: THERE SOON WAS AN AURA OF BEAUTIFUL COLORED LIGHT AROUND HIM, AS IF IT WAS RADIATING FROM HIS HUMAN FORM. AND THEN, SOME GAME ANIMALS STARTED TO SHOW UP UNEXPECTEDLY DURING HIS DAILY CHORES TO DO PATHWAYS, AS IF THEY WANTED THIS GOOD-HEARTED SOUL TO

KILL AND GIVE THEM AWAY AS FOOD GIFTS TO HIS FELLOW SOUL VILLAGERS. AND THIS VERY GOOD-HEARTED MAN DID KILL THOSE GAME ANIMALS THAT HAPPENED TO START SHOWING UP WITH HIM, THE VERY GOOD-HEARTED AND VERY MUCH ALIVE, HELPFUL SOUL. AND WHENEVER THE OTHER SOULS SAW THE MUKLUKS THAT HE WAS WEARING ON HIS FEET, THEY SEEMED ALWAYS TO HAVE SOME VERY UNIDENTIFIED LIGHT ALSO RADIATING OUT FROM THEM. SO THIS VERY GOOD MAN DID HAVE A GOOD REWARD, AND IT DID HAPPEN WHILE HE WAS YET STILL ALIVE BODILY. SOMETHING WAS TELLING HIM THE TRUTH, THAT WHAT HE WAS DOING BY BEING KIND AND ALSO HELPFUL WAS A VERY GOOD DEED, BECAUSE IT ALSO COULD BE SEEN BY HIS FELLOW VILLAGE SOULS THAT WHAT THE GOOD-HEARTED SOUL WAS CARRYING OUT OF HELPING ALL OTHER LIVING SOULS WAS SOMETHING THEY HAD NOT SEEN IN ANY OTHER SOUL BEFORE HIM.

DEMON WANTED SOUL

THIS MAN, WHO HAPPENED TO LOVE DRINKING ALCOHOL, HAPPENED TO BE DOING HIS FAVORITE THING THIS ONE FINE EVENING, AND THAT WAS TO DO SOMETHING THAT THIS VERY ALIVE LIVING SOUL WAS QUITE INTO, AND THAT WAS TO LIVE IT OUT AND CONCENTRATE ON HIS GOOD TIMES, WHICH HE SOMEHOW DID ON A DAILY BASIS. THIS ONE FINE EVENING, HE WAS DOING SOME THING, AND YOU GUESSED RIGHT--HE WAS DOING NONE OTHER THAN THE PARTY HE WAS CARRYING OUT WITH A MUCH-GLADDENED HEAD THAT WAS DIZZY FROM HIS SOMEWHAT ONGOING TRIPS TO BEHIND THAT BIG BUILDING. HE WAS TAKING OR CARRYING IT OUT QUITE SLOWLY, SO THAT THE ALCOHOL WOULD NOT BLACK OUT HIS HEAD TOO QUICKLY, BEFORE HE KNEW WHAT HAD HAPPENED. SO THIS LIVING DRINKING SOUL WAS VERY SLOWLY GETTING TO THAT SOMEWHAT HAPPY LEVEL, SLOWLY BUT SURELY. PLUS, HE WAS ALSO TAKING HIS CHANCES ON SOME OF THE POOL GAMES TO WHICH HE WAS BEING CHALLENGED BY ALL THE OTHER GAMING SOULS WANTING TO DO SOME WINNING AND WHATNOT. AND THIS VERY BODILY ALIVE SOUL HAD, IN FACT,

NOT PASSED OUT, DUE TO ALL OF HIS BEING CAREFUL IN HIS DRINKING THAT VERY SAME NIGHT. WHEN IT WAS GETTING CLOSE TO THIS FUN HOUSE AREA'S HOURS OF BUSINESS CLOSING, THIS PARTIED-UP SOUL DID, IN FACT, MAKE HIS OWN DECISION THAT HE DID HAVE ENOUGH TIME TO DO HIS THING BEHIND THAT BIG BUILDING ONE VERY LAST TIME. SO HE WENT OUTSIDE TO THAT AREA, WHERE HE, THE DRINKING SOUL, HAD A FEELING THAT IT WAS A VERY SAFE SPOT FOR HIM, INDEED. HE GOT HIS BOOTLEGGED JUG FOR HIS VERY MUCH WANTED SWIG. AS HE WAS TAKING HIS SWIG, HE NOTICED SOMETHING WEARING BLACK CLOTHING AND WHICH HAD LONG HAIR, ALSO, THAT WAS SEEN BY THIS VERY LOST SOUL STANDING BESIDE HIM. HE HAD NOT EVEN HEARD HIM APPROACH HIS SPOT, BUT SUDDENLY, IT WAS NOW STANDING BESIDE HIM. SO THIS VERY LOST SOUL ASKED THAT SOMETHING IF HE WANTED A SWIG FROM HIS BOOTLEGGED JUG, ALSO. BUT THAT THING REFUSED HIS OFFER, BUT TOLD HIM THAT HE WANTED TO GIVE THIS SOUL A SWIG FROM HIS JUG. HE TOLD HIM THAT HIS BOTTLE DID NOT HAVE ANY LABELING WHATSOEVER. WHEN THIS DRINKING SOUL LOOKED OVER THIS THING'S JUG THAT HE HAD BEEN TELLING HIM ABOUT, HE NOTICED THAT HIS BOTTLE DID NOT HAVE ANY LABEL ON IT, AND THAT DID GET THIS VERY ALIVE AND WELL SOUL SOMEHOW REALLY SCARED

ALL OF A SUDDEN. THAT MADE HIM REALIZE THAT IF HE DID TAKE ONLY ONE SWIG FROM THAT UNLABELED BOTTLE BEING OFFERED TO HIM FROM THAT VERY EVIL DEMON, HE WOULD END UP VERY MUCH BODILY DEAD. SO HE TOLD THE EVIL DEMON THAT HE HAD HAD ENOUGH TO DRINK ALREADY. AFTER HE HAD TOLD THE BAD EVIL DEMON THAT AND HAPPENED TO LOOK THE OTHER WAY, AND LOOKED AGAIN TOWARDS WHERE THAT THING HAD BEEN STANDING, HE FOUND THAT HE WAS GONE. HE LOOKED AROUND, BUT SAW NO ONE, AND FOUND OUT THAT ONLY HIS FOOTSTEPS WERE VISIBLE IN THE SNOW. AFTER THAT INCIDENT, THIS DRINKING SOUL QUIT HIS BAD DRINKING HABIT, KNOWING THAT IT MAY JUST END HIS LIFE BODILY IF HE KEPT IT UP, AND LET IT DESTROY HIM AND HIS WELL-BEING WHILE HE WAS CARRYING OUT HIS VERY VALUABLE GIFT OF HIS DAILY LIVING, WHICH HE DID LIKE VERY MUCH.

WAS SMALL CHILD

THESE TWO VERY MUCH BODILY ALIVE LIVING SOULS HAPPENED TO BE CARRYING OUT THEIR VERY VALUABLE GIFTS OF THEIR DAILY LIVES IN A SOMEWHAT HARDSHIP-FILLED TOGETHERNESS. THEY ALSO KNEW THAT THEY NO LONGER HAD ANY FOOD TO CONSUME FOR THE CONTINUATION OF THEIR DAILY LIVELIHOOD ACTIVITIES, DUE TO THE SHORTAGE OF FOOD IN THEIR IMMEDIATE AREA, WHICH HAPPENED TO BE OUT IN THE WILDERNESS, MILES AWAY FROM ANY OTHER LIVING SOULS THAT THEY COULD ASK FOR ANY SORT OF HELP FOR THEIR COMING TROUBLE-FILLED DAYS. THE HUSBAND OF THE LADY SOUL HAD NOT RETURNED FROM HIS HUNTING TRIP MONTHS AGO, SO SHE DID KNOW THAT HER MAN WAS DEAD IN BODY, SOMEWHERE OUT IN THE WILDERNESS, DUE TO THE MANY DANGERS THAT WERE VERY COMMON AND DID NOT GIVE OUT SECOND CHANCES FOR ANY OF THE ACTIVE LIVING SOULS WHO WERE CARRYING THEM OUT ON A SOMEWHAT DAILY BASIS. SO THESE TWO VERY ALIVE SOULS KNEW THAT THEY HAD TO HEAD DOWNRIVER FOR HELP, SO THAT THEY MAY NOT HAVE TO END UP BODILY DEAD.

THEY HAPPENED TO DO THE WALK SO THAT THEY MAY HAVE SOMETHING EDIBLE IN THEIR STOMACHES IN ORDER TO SURVIVE. THEY TRAVELED DOWN THAT RIVER BY THE USE OF THEIR LEGS, FOR THEY DID NOT HAVE ANY DOGS, BECAUSE THE MAN HAD TAKEN THEM ALL ON HIS TRIP, FROM WHICH HE WAS NOT TO EVER RETURN, TO SOMEWHERE THAT NOBODY KNEW. THE TWO POOR SOULS HAPPENED TO WALK ALL OF THE DAY ON WHICH THEY HAD STARTED UP EARLY IN THE MORNING. TO THEIR DISAPPOINTMENT, THEY DID NOT EVEN COME ACROSS ANY OTHER SOUL FOR THE BETTER PART OF THEIR JOURNEY DOWN THIS BIG AND WIDE RIVER. AT ABOUT EVENING TIME, THEY SAW A MUD HOUSE WITH SMOKE COMING OUT OF ITS CENTER AREA THAT ALLOWED THE SMOKE TO ESCAPE. UPON SEEING THIS VERY WELCOME SIGHT, THESE TWO VERY ALIVE SOULS QUICKENED THEIR WALK, FOR THEY WERE VERY TIRED AND ALSO HUNGRY. WHEN THEY CAME TO THAT PLACE, THEY ENTERED AND SAW A WOMAN COOKING SOMETHING WITH HER WOODEN POT. BUT SHE HAD A COVER ON IT, SO THESE POOR SOULS DID NOT SEE WHAT SHE HAPPENED TO BE COOKING, DESPITE THE ONGOING SHORTAGE OF FOOD. THIS BAD SOUL INVITED THESE TWO POOR, HUNGRY SOULS FOR DINNER, ALL THE WHILE SAYING WHAT A VERY NICE CHILD THIS WOMAN SOUL HAD. THESE TWO POOR SOULS WERE IN A SOMEWHAT SAFE SPOT, SO

THEY THOUGHT. BUT WHEN THIS VERY BAD
WOMAN SOUL UNCOVERED HER BOILING POT,
THE MOTHER OF THIS SMALL SOUL CHILD
NOTICED A SMALL HUMAN HAND THAT WAS
BEING COOKED BY THIS VERY BAD WOMAN
SOUL. WHEN SHE SAW THAT SMALL HAND,
SHE WAS NO LONGER HUNGRY, BUT WAS
SUDDENLY CONCERNED AND VERY WORRIED
FOR THE SAFTY OF BOTH HER AND HER
VERY MUCH ALIVE SMALL CHILD SOUL. SO
SHE VERY HASTILY TOLD THE BAD WOMAN
SOUL THAT ALL THEY HAD WANTED TO DO
WAS TO REST UP A BIT AT HER PLACE, BUT
WERE READY TO CONTINUE ON THEIR WALK
TO OTHER SETTLEMENTS ALONG THE RIVER.
AND DESPITE THE BAD SOUL'S INVITATION FOR
THEM TO SPEND THE NIGHT AT HER HORROR-
FILLED PLACE, THEY DID GET OUT OF HER
PLACE QUICKLY, AND HEADED DOWNRIVER
TO A MUCH SAFER PLACE, KNOWING THAT
IF THEY HAD SPENT AN EVENING WITH THAT
CANNIBAL, THEY WOULD END UP VERY DEAD
IN BODY.

PICKED ON THE WRONG EVIL THUG

THIS LIVING SOUL, WHO CARRIED OUT VERY BAD DEEDS AND WAS VERY MUCH ALIVE, INDEED, HAPPENED TO LIVE OUT HIS DAILY GIFT OF HIS VERY VALUABLE LIFE JUST TO INFLICT PAIN AND SORROW ON HIS FELLOW MEN ON A NIGHTLY BASIS. HE WAS VERY MUCH INTO MUGGING THE DRUNKS WHO HAPPENED TO BE ON HIS PATH ON ANY GIVEN NIGHT, AND THEREFORE DID NOT KNOW ANY BETTER, DUE TO THEIR DISORIENTED CONDITIONS THAT THEY THEMSELVES HAD GOTTEN INTO BY THEIR OWN FREE WILL, OR BY THE COME-ONS THAT THEY HAD ENCOUNTERED FROM THEIR SO-CALLED BUDDIES OR FRIENDS, FOR THAT MATTER. SO THEN, THIS BAD DEEDS, MUGGING SOUL DID HAVE MANY VICTIMS UNDER HIS BELT, WHO HAD BEEN UNFORTUNATE ENOUGH TO BE ON THE DAILY HIT LIST FOR THIS ROBBER OF THINGS, WHICH WE, THE SOULS ALIVE IN THIS WORLD OF OURS, DO NOT GET ENOUGH OF, OR ALWAYS HAVE A SHORTAGE OF ON A DAILY BASIS, IN OUR ONGOING DAILY GIFTS OF OUR VERY VALUABLE LIVES THAT WE DO CARRY OUT DAILY, DAY IN AND DAY OUT. SO THIS LIVING SOUL WHO CARRIED OUT BAD DEEDS HAD A VERY BAD HABIT. HE RESTED UP

FROM HIS ONGOING, EASY-COME, EASY-GO WORKS DURING THE DAY TIME, WHILE THE REST OF THE HONEST WORLD WAS HARD AT WORK, TRYING THEIR BEST TO MAKE ENDS MEET, SO THAT THEY MAY CONTINUE TO HAVE AVAILABLE FOR THEM WHATEVER LITTLE THAT THEY DO HAVE ON THEIR HANDS ON ANY GIVEN DAY. SO WHAT THIS BAD SOUL WAS INTO WAS VERY WRONG INDEED, BUT HE WAS NOT ABOUT TO GIVE IT UP SO THAT THE REST OF THIS WORLD WOULD INDEED BE A BETTER PLACE TO LIVE IN. HE THEREFORE DID IT DESPITE THE RISKS INVOLVED IN HIS CHOSEN BAD PATHWAY. ON A NIGHTLY BASIS, WEATHER PERMITTING, OR IF HE WAS NOT DOWNED BY SICKNESS, HE DID THESE VERY BAD THINGS BY HIMSELF, THE SOUL THAT DID SOMEWHAT VERY BAD DEEDS, WHO WAS VERY ALIVE AND WELL. SO AS FAR AS HE WAS CONCERNED, HE DID CARE ABOUT HIS OWN SAFTY WHENEVER HE WAS OUT AND ABOUT. SO HE MADE SURE THAT ALL HIS VICTIMS WERE SOMEWHAT MUCH SMALLER THAN HE WAS, OR WERE TOO FAR GONE TO PROTECT THEMSELVES FROM HIS EVIL STRIKING OUT, DUE TO BEING TOO DRUNK TO NOTICE THAT BAD STUFF WAS IN PROGRESS AGAINST THEM, OR NOT HAVING ANY KNOWLEDGE THAT THESE THINGS COULD AND DO HAPPEN TO SOULS THAT CHOOSE TO BE OUT AT NIGHT OR THE WEE HOURS OF VERY EARLY MORNINGS. ONE DAY, WHILE HE WAS OUT

AND ABOUT, CARRYING OUT WHAT HE WAS HOOKED ON VERY MUCH, BOTH PHYSICALLY AND MENTALLY, HE HAPPENED TO SEE A SMALL-SIZED THING ON HIS CHOSEN PATH. THIS VERY SAME NIGHT, WHAT CAME TO THIS BAD SOUL'S MIND VERY LOUDLY AND CLEARLY WAS THAT THIS SMALL-SIZED SOMETHING ON HIS PATH WOULD INDEED BE EASY AS PIE TO GET GOODIES FROM ON THIS SEEMINGLY LUCKY NIGHT FOR HIM, THE SOUL INVOLVED IN VERY BAD DEEDS THOUGHT. SO EVERYTHING WAS ON HIS SIDE THIS NIGHT, AND THERE WERE NO WITNESSES AROUND ANYWHERE THAT COULD WORK AGAINST HIM. WHEN HE GOT WITHIN TOUCHING RANGE OF THE SMALL THING, HE TAPPED THIS SHORT STUFF ON ITS SHOULDER AREA. WHAT TURNED TO FACE HIM SHOCKED HIM VERY MUCH. THE TRENCHCOATED SHORT THING'S FACE LOOKED VERY ROTTEN, AND HE SAW FANGS ON THAT UGLY, UGLY EVIL DEMON'S ROTTED-OUT FACE. WHAT THAT VERY EVIL DEMON DID WAS GRAB THIS POOR BAD SOUL ON HIS LEGS AND HOLD HIM UPSIDE DOWN, AS IF HE DID NOT HAVE ANY WEIGHT AT ALL, FOR HE WAS VERY STRONG, AS FAR AS THE BAD SOUL SAW FOR HIMSELF. WHEN HE HAD DONE SO, THE VERY EVIL DEMON STARTED TO SHAKE THIS POOR BAD SOUL VERY VIOLENTLY. SOMEWHERE ALONG THE LINE, HIS HEAD HIT THE HARD SOIL AND HE PASSED OUT FROM THAT BIG BUMP ON THE GROUND. LATER, AFTER HE

WOKE UP, HE FOUND HE HAD A BIG LUMP ON HIS HEAD. BUT ALL IN ALL, THIS LITTLE BAD INCIDENT CHANGED THIS BAD SOUL INTO A VERY ACTIVE CHURCH MEMBER AFTER HIS VERY BAD NIGHT. HE KNEW THAT YES, EVIL DEMONS DO BAD THINGS AND ARE ALWAYS AROUND, MOSTLY INVISIBLE TO OUR EYES, TO US VERY ALIVE AND ACTIVE SOULS, WHETHER WE CHOOSE TO BE GOOD OR BAD IN OUR DAY-IN AND OUR DAY-OUT ACTIVITIES IN OUR VERY GOOD WORLD IN WHICH SOME THINGS ARE KEPT ON THE HIDDEN SCALE DAILY.

OLD MAN MET LITTLE DEMON IMP

THIS VERY MUCH ALIVE OLD SOUL, WHO
WAS SOMEWHAT INTO HIS MUCH SPENT-OUT
GOLDEN YEARS, DID HAPPENED TO BE OUT
IN THE BEACH AREA OF THIS ONE SMALL
VILLAGE. IN FACT, THE OLD SOUL HAD STARTED
UP HIS VERY MUCH NEEDED LITTLE EXERCISE
WALK QUITE EARLY THAT SAME DAY. THE OLD,
OLD SOUL RESTED ABOUT EACH AND EVERY
MILE OR SO DURING THIS MUCH NEEDED
WALK, IN ORDER FOR HIS ONGOING LITTLE
STRENGTH TO CONTINUE AS IT DID HAPPEN TO
BE WHERE IT WAS AT THAT MOMENT. FOR HIS
MIND WAS FELT BY HIM, THE VERY OLD SOUL,
AS BEING VERY SANE AND STILL VERY CLEAR.
AND THESE ONGOING LITTLE WALKS THAT HE
CARRIED OUT DAILY HELPED THE OLD SOUL
WITH HIS NEED FOR FRESH AIR, AND HELPED
HIM NOT GET SICK, AND HELPED HIM TO STAY
ALIVE AND WELL, AS HE HOPED FOR VERY
MUCH. ON ANY GIVEN DAY, WHEN HE WAS
CARRYING OUT HIS REMAINING DAILY GIFT OF
HIS LIFE, WHICH HE WAS VERY MUCH LIVING
OUT, HE KNEW IN HIS VERY SANE MIND THAT
THERE WOULD NOT BE TOO MANY YEARS LEFT
FOR HIM, THE QUITE VERY OLD SOUL, FOR HE
WAS VERY OLD. AS HE WAS DOING HIS WALK

WITH A PIECE OF STICK TO SUPPORT HIS BODY AS HE TOOK HIS STEPS, HE HAPPENED TO SEE OUT IN THE DISTANCE WHAT SEEMED LIKE A SMALL CHILD, BENT OVER ON THE BEACH'S WATERLINE, DOING SOMETHING THAT THE VERY OLD SOUL DID NOT KNOW WHAT IT WAS. AS HE GOT CLOSER TO THIS CHILD-LIKE FIGURE, HE SAW THAT THING IN QUESTION WAS TRYING TO RETRIEVE SOMETHING FROM THE WATER, AND WAS MAKING LOUD NOISES THAT WERE GRUNTS, COMING NOW AND THEN. THE THING DID NOT EVEN NOTICE HIM WHEN HE HAPPENED TO BE ON THE VERY BACKSIDE OF HIM, IN ORDER TO SEE WHAT THIS LITTLE EVIL DEMON WAS TRYING TO PULL UP. WHAT THIS OLD SOUL NOTICED WAS THAT IT WAS A VERY BIG SALMON, WHICH THIS EVIL LITTLE DEMON HAD SOMEHOW CAUGHT, BUT WAS UNABLE TO PULL ALL THE WAY UP, IN ORDER TO LAND IT ON THE SANDY BEACH. SO THIS VERY OLD SOUL REACHED OVER FROM THE BACKSIDE AREA OF THIS EVIL LITTLE DEMON AND GOT A HOLD OF THAT BIG SALMON, AND PULLED WITH ALL HIS MIGHT. AS HE DID SO, THE SALMON FLEW OVER THEIR HEADS, AND LANDED ON THE SAND FURTHER UP FROM THEIR AREA OF LABORING. THE LITTLE EVIL DEMON LANDED ON HIS BACK AFTER HE HAD FALLEN BACKWARDS AND WAS NOW LOOKING UP AT THE VERY OLD LIVING SOUL WITH VERY WIDE OPEN FEAR-FILLED EYES. HIS MOUTH, WHICH WAS FILLED WITH MANY TEETH, WAS

ALSO WIDE OPEN. THESE TWO LOOKED AT EACH OTHER FOR A WHOLE MINUTE OR SO, AND AFTER SEEING THAT THE OLD LIVING SOUL MEANT HIM NO HARM, THE LITTLE UGLY EVIL THING SAT UP AND FACED THE VERY OLD SOUL, ALL THE WHILE BRUSHING THE SAND FROM HIS LONG-FINGERNAILED LITTLE HANDS. HE TOLD THIS VERY OLD SOUL THAT HE WOULD GRANT HIM THREE WISHES FOR ALL HIS TROUBLES, SMILING VERY EVILLY ALL THE WHILE. WHAT THIS VERY OLD SOUL WISHED FOR IN HIS MIND WAS FOR TEN MORE YEARS TO BE ADDED TO HIS DAILY GIFT OF LIFE, FOR HIS STRENGTH TO NOT LET HIM DOWN, AND FOR HIS STOMACH TO BE FULL ON A DAILY BASIS. AFTER ALL HAD BEEN SAID AND DONE, THE LITTLE EVIL DEMON RETRIEVED THAT BIG SALMON AND DISAPPEARED RIGHT BEFORE THAT OLD SOUL'S EYES, ALONG WITH THAT SALMON THAT HE HAD SOMEHOW CAUGHT. AS THE OLD SOUL WALKED BACK TO HIS VILLAGE, HE DID FEEL STRONGER IN BODY AND WAS NOT A BIT TIRED AS HE HAD BEEN BEFORE, BUT SEEMED TO BE, AS HE NOTICED, MUCH, MUCH HEALTHIER.

EVIL DEMON'S WONDERING SOUL

THIS ONE MAN LIVING SOUL, WHO LIVED IN THIS ONE SMALL VILLAGE, HAPPENED TO HAVE A NOT-SO-BRIGHT HABIT, WHICH WAS TO USE HIS MIND TO THINK ABOUT A LOT OF THINGS. HE CARRIED OUT HIS VERY THING TO DO SOME THOUGHT WORK ON SOME OF THE UNSEEN THINGS OF THIS SOMETIMES VERY GOOD WORLD OF OURS. THOSE THINGS ON HIS MIND, WHICH WAS VERY SANE INDEED, WERE ABOUT THOSE EVIL INVISIBLE DEMONS THAT DO NOT, UNDER ANY CIRCUMSTANCES, TRY TO HELP ANY VERY ALIVE SOUL. THEY ARE THE VERY OPPOSITE OF GOOD, AND ARE, IN TRUTH, WORKING VERY HARD AND HAVE A DUTY TO DO US GREAT HARM TWENTY-FOUR HOURS A DAY, SEVEN DAYS A WEEK, WITHOUT A SINGLE REST. BUT THEY ARE WORKING VERY HARD TO DO EVERY HUMAN ALIVE GREAT HARM, FOR THEY HATE EVERY SOUL ALIVE AND ARE ALWAYS WISHING THAT THEY WERE HUMAN. THAT IS A LITTLE PART OF THE CAUSE FOR WHY THEY, THE VERY EVIL, UGLY, MULTI-TOOTHED DEMONS, WITH VERY BAD ODORS COMING FROM WITHIN THEIR SUPERNATURAL FORMS, HATE EVERY SOUL NOW ALIVE AND WELL VERY PASSIONATELY,

AND VERY TRUTHFULLY. ANYWAY, THIS POOR WONDERING TYPE OF A LIVING AND VERY ALIVE SOUL USED HIS VERY VALUABLE GIFE OF HIS DAILY LIFE WONDERING WHAT THESE VERY EVIL THINGS LOOKED LIKE OR WHAT THEY DID CARRY OUT DAILY, FOR HE HAD NOT SEEN ANY AROUND LATELY. IT SEEMED TO HIM THAT HE WASN'T ABOUT TO MEET ANY ONE OF THEM ONE-ON-ONE ANYTIME SOON. BUT HE DECIDED ONE DAY THAT HE WOULD VISIT HIS DEAR OLD DAD, WHO WAS LIVING IN ANOTHER VILLAGE, LOCATED ABOUT THIRTY MILES AWAY FROM HIS HOMETOWN VILLAGE. SO HE VISITED HIS DAD THAT SAME DAY. WHEN HE GOT TO HIS DAD'S VILLAGE, HE CHAINED UP HIS DOGS AND DID WHATEVER NEEDED TO BE DONE BEFORE ENTERING HIS HOUSE. THAT SAME NIGHT, HIS FATHER TOLD HIM THAT HE COULD SLEEP IN HIS BED, FOR HE HAD PLANNED TO SPEND THE NIGHT AT HIS DAUGHTER'S HOUSE, DUE TO HER HUSBAND BEING OUT ON A CAMPING TRIP WITH HIS FRIENDS, HUNTING GAME. AFTER THIS WONDERING-MINDED LIVING SOUL HAD EATEN AT HIS SISTER'S HOUSE, HE WENT BACK TO HIS DAD'S HOUSE, SO THAT HE COULD REST HIS VERY TIRED AND SORE BODY. HE WAS TIRED AND SORE DUE TO THAT DOG TEAM RIDE, WHICH HE HAD CARRIED OUT IN ORDER TO SEE HIS VERY MUCH LOVED DAD. AS HE LAY DOWN ON HIS DAD'S BED, HE HEARD HIS DOOR OPEN UP, AND ALSO HEARD FOOTSTEPS COMING TOWARDS HIS DAD'S

ROOM. THE BAD SIDE WAS THAT WHEN THE DOOR OF HIS DAD'S HOUSE OPENED UP, HE COULD NO LONGER MOVE, BUT LAY VERY STIFFLY ON HIS DAD'S BED. WHEN ALL OF THESE VERY ODD THINGS HAPPENED TO HIM, THE WONDERING-MINDED LIVING SOUL WAS SUDDENLY VERY SCARED, AND FELT VERY COLD, BODILY. HIS BODY WAS TINKLING ALL OVER FROM ALL THAT WAS HAPPENING AT THAT VERY MOMENT. WHEN THAT EVIL THING GOT TO HIS DAD'S BEDROOM DOOR, HE TOLD HIM WITH HIS VERY EVIL-SOUNDING VOICE THAT HE HAD COME TO SHOW HIM WHAT THEY, THE EVIL DEMONS, WERE ALL ABOUT, SINCE HE HAD BEEN THINKING AND HAD BEEN WONDERING IN HIS MIND ABOUT THEM. THEN THE EVIL DEMON CAME AND SAT ON HIS BODY, AND HIS WEIGHT WAS VERY HEAVY. WHEN HE, THE EVIL THING, SAT ON HIM, IT WAS SOMEWHERE OVER FIVE HUNDRED POUNDS ON HIS SUPERNATURAL FORM, AND VERY BAD ODORS WERE COMING FROM HIS, THE VERY EVIL DEMON'S, FORM. AFTER ONLY A SHORT TIME WITH THIS POOR SOUL, THE EVIL THING WITH VERY BAD ODORS COMING FROM WITHIN HIS FORM LEFT, AND THIS WONDERING POOR SOUL SUDDENLY STARTED MOVING AFTER THE EVIL THING WAS GONE. BUT THOSE VERY BAD ODORS WERE SENSED BY THIS POOR SOUL FOR THREE WHOLE DAYS AFTERWARDS. WHAT THIS POOR WONDERING SOUL DID FIND OUT THAT DAY WAS THAT

THE EVIL DEMONS WERE VERY BAD-ODORED AND WERE ALSO VERY STRONG AND VERY HEAVY, ALSO. HE FOUND OUT THAT THEY WERE OUT TO DO HARM AND NOT GOOD TO EVERY SOUL THAT WOULD LISTEN TO THEIR SUPERNATUALLY INVISIBLE VOICES, WHICH THE SOULS OF THIS WORLD CANNOT HEAR. BUT THEY ARE DOING SO, VERY HIDDEN, FOR THEY ARE VERY INVISIBLE TO THE EYES OF EVERY SOUL ALIVE UP TO THIS VERY DAY. BUT THEY ARE, WITH EVERY SOUL, DAY IN AND DAY OUT, EVERY DAY, DOING GREAT HARM TO US DAILY, AS WE CONTINUE TO CARRY OUT OUR PRECIOUS, VERY VALUABLE GIFT OF OUR DAILY LIVES THAT ARE GIVEN TO US VERY FREELY.

CRIPPLED MAN'S REVENGE

THERE HAPPENED TO LIVE A POOR SOUL WHO HAPPENED TO BE LIVING OUT HIS VERY PRECIOUS DAILY GIFT OF HIS REQUIRED BREATH--IN THIS CASE, HIS DAILY GIFT OF LIFE. THIS POOR, POOR LIVING SOUL HAD A SOMEWHAT BAD SETBACK, AS MOST OF HIS FELLOW MEN DID VERY MUCH KNOW. IN THE SMALL VILLAGE HE WAS BORN INTO IN THIS SOMETIMES GOOD WORLD OF OURS, THIS POOR SOUL IN QUESTION WAS LABELED AS BEING HELPLESS, DUE TO BEING CRIPPLED. HE HAD ONLY ONE GOOD ARM THAT HAPPENED TO BE IN GOOD CONDITION STILL, BUT NOT ALL OF THE VERY ALIVE AND WELL-LIVING SOULS FELT SORRY FOR THIS POOR OLD SOUL. THERE WAS THESE TWO INDIVIDUALS THAT DID NOT EVEN FEEL SORRY FOR HIM, FOR THEY DID NOT KNOW ANY BETTER. THESE TWO WERE IN FACT QUITE YOUNG IN AGE; THEREFORE, WHAT THESE TWO QUITE YOUNG LIVING SOULS HAD WAS A VERY BAD HABIT. THAT BAD HABIT OF THESE TWO VERY YOUNG SOULS WAS TO MAKE SURE THAT THIS POOR, POOR CRIPPLED SOUL'S DAYS WERE NOT FULL OF HAPPINESS, BUT VERY MUCH HARDER ALL THE MORE. DURING THIS POOR SOUL'S ONGOING DAILY EXISTENCE,

AS HE WAS DOING HIS VERY BEST TO MAKE HIS DAILY GIFT OF HIS CONTINUING DAILY LIFE A LITTLE MORE TROUBLE-FREE, THESE TWO VERY YOUNG LIVING SOULS WOULD OFTEN POKE HOLES IN THIS POOR HELPLESS SOUL'S MUD HOUSE, AND WOULD HOUND HIM, THE POOR HELPLESS SOUL, DAILY, BY CALLING HIM NAMES. MORE OFTEN THAN NOT, THEY WOULD TRIP HIM AND MAKE HIM FALL DOWN ON THE DIRT ON A DAILY BASIS, AND WOULD OFTEN BREAK UP HIS CANE AFTER GETTING IT WHILE HE WAS WALKING ABOUT HIS HOME VILLAGE. THEY GOT IT BY COMING UP ON HIM FROM BEHIND HIM, FROM HIS BACK SIDE, AFTER LAYING IN THE TALL GRASS, HIDDEN FROM HIM. SO THIS POOR HELPLESS SOUL HAD BIG PROBLEMS BEING ADDED BY THESE TWO BAD YOUNG SOULS TO ALL HIS OTHER PROBLEMS THAT HE HAPPENED TO HAVE ON HIS HANDS AT THAT PERIOD IN TIME. ONE DAY, THIS POOR SOUL THOUGHT TO HIMSELF THAT ENOUGH WAS ENOUGH. SO THEN, HE THEREFORE PAID A SHAMAN WITH SOME FOOD THAT HAD BEEN GIVEN TO HIM BY SOME OF THE VILLAGE'S GOOD HUNTERS OF BIG GAME. THE POOR CRIPPED HELPLESS SOUL PAID THIS SHAMAN TO PUT A HEX ON THESE TWO YOUNG TROUBLE-MAKERS. WHAT HAPPENED AFTERWARDS WAS THIS: EVERY TIME THESE TWO VERY YOUNG TROUBLE-MAKING YOUNG SOULS TRIED THEIR CHOICE TO MAKE THIS POOR CRIPPLED SOUL'S DAYS MUCH MORE TROUBLESOME,

THEY WOULD START TO FEEL REALLY HOT AND BURNING SENSATIONS WOULD BE FELT ALL OVER THEIR YOUNG BODIES. FOR THE REAL TRUTH TO BE REALIZED BY ALL, THESE TWO POOR YOUNG TROUBLED SOULS, SOMEWHERE INSIDE OF THEIR YOUNG HEADS, WOULD START TO YELL AND SCREAM, AND START TO CRY REALLY LOUDLY, SEEMINGLY FOR NO APPARENT REASON AT ALL. THESE TWO YOUNG SOULS DID COME TO THE CONCLUSION THAT EACH AND EVERY TIME THAT THEY TRIED TO CARRY OUT THEIR FORMER INVOLVEMENT IN MAKING THE POOR, CRIPPLED SOUL'S LIFE A LITTLE HARDER, THESE UNEXPLAINABLE BURNING SENSATIONS WOULD THEN BE FELT BY THE TWO OF THEM, ALL OVER THEIR YOUNG BODIES, AND MORE OFTEN THAN NOT, THEY WOULD START CRYING AND YELLING OUT REALLY LOUDLY THAT THEY WERE BURNING UP. AFTER REALIZING THAT THEY COULD NO LONGER CARRY OUT THEIR TROUBLE-MAKING ABILITIES, THESE TWO YOUNG, NOT-SO-EXCELLENT LIVING SOULS QUIT THEIR BAD MISTAKES. AFTERWARDS, THEY STARTED TO HELP OUT THIS POOR, HELPLESS CRIPPLED SOUL, WANTING HIM TO FORGIVE THEM FOR THEIR FORMER TRIES TO MAKE HIS LIFE VERY MISERABLE FOR HIM, THE POOR, HELPLESS, VERY ALIVE SOUL, WHO WAS NOW IN A MUCH BETTER STAGE AND CONDITION, WITH THE HELP OF THAT SHAMAN TO GET THE JOB DONE.

HOOTER DEMONS

THIS MAN WANTED TO CAPTURE A DEMON, TO THEREFORE MAKE SOME WISHES TO HIS ADVANTAGE, SO THAT HE COULD MAKE HIS SOMEWHAT HARD LIFE A LITTLE EASIER FOR HIMSELF. HE LIVED OUT HIS DAILY EXISTENCE IN THIS ONE SMALL VILLAGE. THIS VERY MUCH BODILY ALIVE LIVING SOUL OF A MAN, WHO WANTED TO EXECUTE SOME SEEMINGLY VERY VALUBLE WISHES, ASKED AROUND HIS HOME VILLAGE ABOUT WHETHER ANY OF HIS FELLOW SOULS HAPPENED TO KNOW ANY AREAS IN HIS HOME VILLAGE'S PERIMETER WHERE THESE VERY EVIL CREATURES MAY BE READILY AVAILABLE, OR HAD BEEN SPOTTED BY THEM. THIS FELLOW, A VERY MUCH ALIVE SOUL, WAS TOLD BY ONE OF THE SOULS THAT HE HAD HEARD SOME VERY STRANGE HOOTING SOUNDS IN THIS ONE PARTICULAR AREA UPRIVER FROM THEIR HOME SPOT. BUT HE ALSO STATED AND CAUTIONED THE LIVING SOUL WHO WANTED TO MAKE WISHES THAT THESE EVIL CREATURES WERE VERY BAD, AND DANGEROUS TO MESS AROUND WITH, FOR THEY WERE SUPERNATURAL EVIL BEINGS AND HAD BEEN AROUND EVER SINCE THE WORLD WAS CREATED. THE OTHER SOUL

TOLD HIM SO, BUT ALL IN ALL, THIS LIVING SOUL WANTING TO MAKE SOME WISHES MADE HIS PLANS TO CHECK OUT THIS AREA WHERE THOSE VERY STRANGE SOUNDS INDEED HAD BEEN HEARD BY THIS OTHER INFORMATIVE LIVING SOUL. SO THEN, THIS WISHFUL SOUL DID MAKE HIS TRIP, WHICH HE SOMEWHAT WANTED TO CARRY OUT, TO THE AREA HE HAD BEEN TOLD OF BY THIS OTHER SOUL. HE MADE A HIDEOUT, CONSISTING OF SOME TREE BRANCHS, WHICH HE GATHERED FOR THE PURPOSE OF CONCEALING HIMSELF FROM ALL THAT WAS EVER CREATED IN THIS VERY GOOD WORLD OF OURS, CALLED THE EARTH BY ALL ALIVE AND WELL LIVING SOULS, SO TO SPEAK. HE WAS HIDDEN FROM EVERYTHING ALL DAY, AND NO DEMONS APPEARED ANYWHERE NEAR HIS HIDEOUT. BUT AS THE SUN WAS JUST STARTING TO SET ON HIS WEST SIDE, HE HEARD SOMETHING UNEARTHLY FROM THE AREA DOWNRIVER FROM HIS HIDDEN POSITION'S LOCATION, WHERE HE HAPPENED TO BE MAKING THE MISTAKE OF HIS LIFETIME. HE SPOTTED THIS VERY EVIL CREATURE COMING UPRIVER ON THE RIVERBANK, ISSUING OUT THOSE UNEARTHLY CRIES OF HIS EVERY NOW AND THEN. WHEN THIS VERY EVIL THING GOT WITHIN ABOUT FIFTEEN FEET OR SO, THIS POOR WISHFUL SOUL SHOT THAT EVIL CREATURE WITH HIS TWELVE-GAUGE, SINGLE SHOT SHOTGUN, HOPING THAT IT WOULD DISABLE THE THING

SO THAT HE COULD CAPTURE HIM. HE DID VERY MUCH WANT TO DO SO, BUT AS SOON AS HE HAD SHOT THE VERY EVIL DEMON, THIS POOR LIVING SOUL LOST CONTACT OF HIS SENSES. IN OTHER WORDS, HIS MIND BECAME BLANK. WHEN HE CAME TO, HE REALIZED HE WAS WALKING SOMEWHERE WITHOUT HIS BOOTS, BUT HE BLACKED OUT AGAIN, ONLY AFTER A SHORT MOMENT. NEXT, WHEN HE FINALLY HAD GAINED HIS CONSCIOUSNESS, IT WAS ALREADY MORNING TIME. THEN, WHEN HE, THE POOR WISHFUL SOUL, LOOKED AROUND, HE SAW HIS SHOTGUN, MINUS ITS STOCK. ITS GUN BARREL PART WAS ALSO BENT UP. HE ALSO NOTICED THAT HE WAS NOT WEARING HIS BOOTS, BUT WAS BAREFOOT. ALSO, HE WAS ABOUT FIFTEEN MILES AWAY FROM HIS FORMER HIDEOUT. WHAT THIS POOR WISHFUL SOUL REALIZED WAS THAT THOSE VERY EVIL BEINGS WERE IMPOSSIBLE TO GAIN ACCESS TO, AND HE NOW KNEW THAT IT WAS VERY DANGEROUS TO MESS WITH THEM, FOR THEY WERE NOT HUMAN, WITH HUMAN BODIES, BUT WERE SUPERNATURAL CREATURES WITH VERY EVIL INTENTIONS THAT THEY, THE EVIL BEINGS, WANT TO INFLICT ON EVERY SOUL ALIVE IN OUR WORLD TODAY. THEY WERE VERY HIDDEN AND ALSO INVISIBLE, SO THAT WE MAY NOT SEE HOW VERY EVIL AND HIDEOUS THEY ARE.

VERY STRANGE VISITOR

THIS MAN AND HIS VERY MUCH LOVED WIFE AND SOMEWHAT LONG-TIME COMPANION CARRIED OUT THEIR DAILY GIFTS OF THEIR VERY VALUBLE LIVES, HELPING EACH OTHER OUT ON A DAILY BASIS, IN THIS VERY GOOD WORLD OF OURS. THESE TWO VERY ALIVE AND WELL-LIVING SOULS WHO LOVED EACH OTHER WERE OUT IN THE WILDERNESS IN THEIR CAMPING PLACE, GATHERING FOOD THAT THEY KNEW WOULD HELP THEM OUT THAT WINTER. ONE DAY AFTER COMING BACK TO THEIR CAMPSITE, THEY, THE TWO LOVING SOULS, SAT TOGETHER FOR THEIR MUCH NEEDED EVENING MEAL. AFTER THEIR VERY SATISFYING MEAL, THE MAN SOUL TOLD HIS WIFE THAT HE WAS GOING OUT TO MAKE A STEAMBATH FOR THE TWO OF THEM SO THAT THEY COULD HAVE A CHANCE TO CLEAN THE ACCUMULATED DIRT, GRIME, AND SWEAT OFF THEIR VERY MUCH ALIVE BODIES. WHEN ALL HAD BEEN SAID AND DONE, THESE TWO SOULS STARTED THEIR MUCH NEEDED WASH-UP INSIDE THE VERY WARMED-UP SWEATHOUSE THAT THEY, THE TWO SOULS, HAPPENED TO OWN. SOME TIME LATER, DURING THEIR VERY MUCH NEEDED WASHING-UP SESSION,

THESE TWO SOULS HEARD A WOMAN'S VOICE JUST OUTSIDE THEIR SWEATHOUSE, WHICH WAS BUILT USING DRIFTWOOD AND MUD. THE VOICE ASKED THEM IF SHE COULD JOIN THEM DURING THEIR SOMEWHAT HAPPY HOUR. THEY TOLD THAT LADY THE TRUTH, THAT SHE WAS VERY WELCOME TO DO SO. THESE TWO LOVING SOULS WERE NOT TOO CONCERNED THAT THEY HAD NOT EVER SEEN THIS WOMAN BEFORE IN THEIR ENTIRE LIVES, NOR WERE THEY ASKING TOO MANY QUESTIONS ABOUT WHO SHE WAS OR WHERE SHE HAD SUDDENLY APPEARED FROM. THEY WELCOMED HER JUST THE SAME. AFTER SOME TIME HAD PASSED INSIDE THAT VERY WARMED-UP SWEATHOUSE FOR THESE THREE, THE WIFE OF THIS MAN SOUL HAPPENED TO LOOK TOWARDS THEIR INVITED GUEST, AND SHE NOTICED SOMETHING VERY STRANGE, INDEED, ABOUT THAT WOMAN THAT THEY THEMSELVES HAD INVITED TO JOIN THEM, THE TWO VERY LOVING SOULS. WHAT THIS WOMEN SOUL SAW WAS THIS: THE INVITED LADY WAS FLOATING ON AIR AND WAS SUSPENDED IN THE AIR ABOUT TWO INCHES OR SO FROM THEIR SWEATBATH BUILDING'S GRASS-COVERED DIRT FLOOR. SO SHE, THE WIFE OF THIS MAN SOUL, NUDGED HIM ON HIS SHOULDER AND POINTED HER FINGER TOWARDS THIS LADY THAT WAS WITH THEM AT THAT VERY MOMENT. WHAT THE HUSBAND SAW WAS THAT THIS WELCOMED GUEST OF THEIRS WAS INDEED FLOATING ON AIR. THAT

WAS WHEN HE, THE MAN SOUL WHO LOVED HIS WIFE VERY MUCH, MOTIONED TO HIS WIFE THAT THEY SHOULD BOTH LEAVE, AND THEY GOT OUT OF THEIR MUD SWEATHOUSE RIGHT AWAY WITHOUT SO MUCH AS ANY TALK BEING EXCHANGED BY THE THREE OF THEM. THESE TWO LOVING SOULS LEFT THAT HOT AND VERY WARMED-UP STRUCTURE, AND PUT ON THEIR FUR GARMENTS WITHOUT EVEN HAVING A CHANCE TO DRY OFF THEIR BODIES FIRST. RIGHT AWAY, THESE TWO VERY MUCH ALIVE AND WELL-LIVING SOULS, WHO LOVED EACH OTHER VERY MUCH, HURRIEDLY AND HASITLY RETRIEVED WHAT LITTLE THEY HAPPENED TO CALL THEIR BELONGINGS FROM THEIR MUD-BUILT HOUSE, AND LOADED UP THEIR KAYAK WITH THEM, SO THAT THEY COULD GET AWAY FROM THEIR CAMPSITE AND AWAY FROM THAT VERY STRANGE THING THAT OCCURRED DURING THEIR VERY MUCH NEEDED SWEATHOUSE TIME-OUT. WHAT THESE TWO LOVING SOULS DID WAS GO BACK TO THEIR HOME VILLAGE, WHERE THEY KNEW THAT THEY WOULD SOMEHOW BE IN A MUCH SAFER PLACE.

MAD BOX-SHAPED DEMON MET

THIS SMALL VILLAGE MEMBER SOUL WAS IN THE PROCESS OF DOING HIS RETURN TRIP FROM HIS DAY OUT IN THE UNFORGIVING WILDERNESS ON THIS VERY DAY, WHICH WAS QUITE COLD OUTDOORS. THAT VERY SAME DAY INDEED, THIS VILLAGE MEMBER SOUL WAS CARRYING OUT HIS WALK QUITE BRISKLY, TAKING LONG STEPS ALL THE WHILE, DUE TO THE VERY FACT THAT THE NIGHTTIME DARKNESS WAS CLOSING IN ON HIM, THE WALKING LIVING SOUL, QUITE QUICKLY, MUCH TO HIS DISMAY. HE ALSO WANTED TO BE BACK AT HIS HOME SPOT BEFORE THE WOLVES IN HIS VILLAGE'S AREA CAME OUT TO HUNT FOR THEMSELVES AND THEIR EVER-HUNGRY FAMILY GROUPS. AND HE, THE HUNTING SOUL, WAS FEELING QUITE SCARED OF THEM, KNOWING IN HIS MIND THAT THESE WILD ANIMALS HAD KILLED AND CONSUMED SOME OF HIS FORMER VILLAGE MEMBER SOULS ONCE IN A WHILE, IF THEY HAPPENED TO BE TAKING SOME UNREVERSABLE RIGHTS WHILE THEY WERE YET STILL AMONG THE VERY ALIVE AND WELL SOULS OF HIS HOME VILLAGE. SO DURING THE COURSE QUICKLY WALKING BACK TO HIS VILLAGE, THIS SOUL

HAPPENED TO SEE SOMETHING ON THE MAIN TRAIL THAT HE WAS NOW WALKING ON, WHICH WAS OFTEN USED BY HIS FELLOW SOULS TO TRAVEL ON DAILY, DAY IN AND DAY OUT, EVERY DAY. AS THIS SOUL GOING HOME GOT CLOSER AND CLOSER TO THAT THING, WHICH WAS ALSO DOING HIS OWN THING ON THE MAIN TRAIL, HE NOTICED THAT IT WAS SQUARE-SHAPED, AND THAT MADE THIS VERY POOR SOUL'S HEART BEAT IN A MUCH FASTER MODE. THE OTHER UNUSUAL THING WAS THAT THIS SOMETHING WAS VERY SHORT. AND WHAT THIS SOUL THAT WAS ALIVE NOW KNEW IN HIS VERY SANE MIND WAS THAT IT WAS AN EVIL DEMON THAT HE WAS ABOUT TO MEET HEAD-ON, BUT ALL THE MORE, HE DID NOT SLACK OFF HIS WALKING PACE, ALTHOUGH SOME HARM COULD BE AWAITING HIM WHEN HE MET UP WITH THAT UGLY, LITTLE EVIL DEMON NOW GETTING QUITE CLOSE TO HIM, THE VILLAGE MEMBER, WHO WAS A LIVING, BODILY ALIVE SOUL. HE WAS MUCH MORE AFRAID OF THE WOLVES, FOR WITHOUT A DOUBT THEY WOULD BE OUT AND ABOUT THAT VERY SAME NIGHT, HUNTING FOR SOMETHING THAT THEY COULD KILL AND THEREFORE EAT. WHEN THIS TRAVELING SOUL GOT WITHIN ABOUT TWENTY FEET OR SO OF THIS ONCOMING SQUARE-FORMED, VERY EVIL LITTLE DEMON, THE VILLAGER SOUL ADDRESSED THE EVIL CREATURE IN THIS MANNER (AND QUITE LOUDLY, ALSO): "HEY, YOU UGLY BEAST." HE DID

THAT BECAUSE THE SHORT SQUARE-SHAPED EVIL BEAST HAD VERY EVIL-LOOKING EYES, WHICH WERE ALSO GLOWING RED. ALSO, HIS MOUTH, WHICH WAS EVILLY-FORMED, WAS STRETCHED FROM EAR TO EAR ON HIS VERY EVIL-LOOKING SCARY FACE. THEN HE SAID THIS VERY QUOTE TO THAT CREATURE: "WHAT IN THE NAME OF HELL ARE YOU BLOCKING MY TRAIL FOR? THIS IS MY TRAIL AND NOT YOURS." THAT WAS WHEN THAT EVIL BEAST GOT REALLY MAD AT THAT TRAVELING-HOME SOUL AND AS HE, THE EVIL DEMON, STEPPED ASIDE FROM THAT MAIN TRAIL, HE SAID TO THAT GOING-HOME SOUL WITH HIS VERY EVIL-SOUNDING VOICE, "WHO DO YOU THINK YOU ARE? YOU ARE NOTHING BUT AN AGED, STINKING FOOD-EATER, AND YOU WILL AMOUNT TO NOTHING, EVEN IF YOU HAPPEN TO STILL BE ALIVE AMONG YOUR FELLOW SOULS FOR A HUNDRED MORE YEARS. YOUR OTHER PROBLEM IS THAT YOU DO NOT EVEN OWN A DOGTEAM LIKE YOUR OTHER SO-CALLED FRIENDS." AND THAT GOING-HOME SOUL FELT MUCH HAPPIER, KNOWING THAT NOW HE WAS GOING TO REACH HIS HOME VILLAGE QUITE SAFE AND STILL IN ONE PIECE THAT VERY SAME NIGHT, AFTER FINDING OUT THAT EVIL-FACED CREATURE WAS NOW TOO MAD TO DO ANYTHING HARMFUL TO HIM, THE VILLAGER SOUL, WHO WAS GOING HOME THAT DAY FROM HIS ALL-DAY HUNTING TRIP OUT IN THE VERY UNFORGIVING WILDERNESS.

SCARED WITLESS

ONE DAY, A MAN WITH A SOUL WENT OUT
ON A HUNTING TRIP QUITE FAR FROM HIS
HOME VILLAGE. THIS VERY UNLUCKY SOUL
WAS OUT IN THE WILDERNESS, HUNTING
FOOD FOR HIS CURRENT FAMILY MEMBERS,
WHOM HE HAPPENED TO BE SUPPORTING WITH
HIS SOMEWHAT GOOD HUNTING SKILLS. AND
HE, THE VERY UNLUCKY SOUL, HAPPENED TO
BE OUT THAT DAY, USING HIS DOGTEAM TO
DO ALL THAT NEEDED TO BE CARRIED OUT
BY HIM BY HIS VERY OWN FREE WILL AND
POWER. THE BAD THING WAS THAT HE, THE
POOR SOUL, HAD TRAVELED QUITE FAR FROM
HIS HOME SPOT, AND THE NIGHT'S DARKNESS
CAME AROUND QUITE EARLY IN THE EVENING
HOURS, DUE TO THE SHORTNESS OF DAYLIGHT
HOURS DURING THE WINTER MONTHS. AFTER
TRAVELING ALL DAY TO HIS HUNTING AREA,
WHICH HE HAD NOT EVEN REACHED THAT
DAY THAT WAS VERY BAD FOR HIM AND HIM
ALONE, THIS POOR, UNLUCKY SOUL HAPPENED
TO REACH THIS SMALL MUD STEAMHOUSE
THAT HAD BEEN BUILT BY SOMEONE. AND
UPON REACHING THIS SEEMINGLY VERY
SAFE PLACE TO SPEND HIS NIGHT, HE, THE
POOR, POOR SOUL, UNHITCHED HIS DOGTEAM

AND TIED UP HIS VERY TIRED DOGS TO SOME NEARBY TREES IN THAT SAME AREA. AFTER FEEDING HIS HUNGRY DOGS, HE READIED HIMSELF TO SPEND HIS NIGHT INSIDE THAT MUD STEAMHOUSE, AFTER BRINGING IN HIS SLEEPING GEAR AND HIS 30-30 WINCHESTER RIFLE. HE ALSO BROUGHT IN THE FOOD THAT HIS DEAR WIFE HAD PREPARED FOR HIM FOR HIS HUNTING TRIP. AFTER LIGHTING UP THE STOVE, HE ATE SOME OF THE FOOD THAT HIS WIFE HAD PREPARED FOR HIM. AFTER HIS MEAL THAT CONSISTED OF SOME DRIED MEAT AND SEAL OIL, AS THIS VERY ALIVE, UNLUCKY SOUL WAS GETTING HIMSELF READY FOR HIS NIGHT'S REST, HE HAPPENED TO HEAR HIS DOGS BEING DISTURBED BY SOMETHING THAT HE COULD NOT, UNDER ANY CIRCUMSTANCES, RECOGNIZE. THINKING THAT IT MAY HAVE BEEN SOME WILD ANIMAL, HE WAS NOT WORRIED TOO MUCH ABOUT THAT DISTURBANCE OF HIS DOGS AT THAT VERY MOMENT, SINCE HE WAS VERY TIRED FROM HIS ALL-DAY TRAVELING THAT VERY SAME DAY. AFTER A SHORT PERIOD OF TIME, HE HEARD SOMETHING GOING ON THAT SMALL STEAMHOUSE'S PORCH. HE BECAME HAPPY, THINKING TO HIMSELF THAT HE HAD A GUEST THAT HE WAS VERY READY TO RELATE TO. THEN, WHEN THE DOOR OPENED UP TO THE INSIDE AREA OF THAT SMALL MUD STEAMHOUSE THAT HE, THE POOR UNLUCKY SOUL, WAS IN, HE SAW WITH HIS VERY OWN EYES WHAT IT WAS. IT WAS A BIG, HAIRY HAND,

WITH VERY LONG, CLAW-LIKE FINGERNAILS ATTATCHED TO IT. AFTER REALIZING WHAT IT WAS, TOTAL SHOCK SET IN TO THIS POOR SOUL'S MIND AND BODY. HE LOST ALL HIS MOVEMENT MECHANISMS; ALSO HE, THE POOR SOUL, FELT VERY HELPLESS AND QUITE LOST AND ALONE. AT THAT VERY BAD MOMENT FOR HIM, THAT EVILLY-CLAWED HAND, NO DOUBT CONTROLLED BY SOME EVIL DEMON, CAME IN VERY SLOWLY TOWARD THIS POOR, POOR UNLUCKY SOUL, THEN PROCEEDED TO CLIMB UP ON HIS BODY. AFTER IT HAD REACHED HIS VERY UNMOVING BODY, IT MADE ITS WAY TOWARDS HIS NECK. DURING THIS, WHEN THAT FRIGHTENING HAND HAD REACHED THIS POOR SOUL'S SHOULDER AREA, THE POOR SOUL TURNED HIS HEAD SIDEWAYS AND BIT THAT VERY FRIGHTENING HAND. AND WHEN HE BIT THAT EVIL, CLAWED HAND, THE POOR SOUL SMELLED VERY FOUL ODORS COMING FROM THAT VERY FRIGHTENING HAND. THAT EVIL, DEMON-CONTROLLED CLAW LET OUT AN UNEARTHLY SCREAM, AS IF FROM SOME GREAT PAIN. THEN IT RUSHED DOWN FROM THIS POOR SOUL'S BODY, OPENED THE DOOR, AND THEN RUSHED OUT, WITH SOUNDS OF VERY QUICKLY MOVING FEET. IT SLAMMED THE DOOR SHUT BEHIND IT. AS SOON AS IT WAS GONE, THE POOR SOUL STARTED MOVING SUDDENLY. THEN THE POOR SOUL GOT HIS GUN AND WENT OUT, FIRING HIS WEAPON, REALLY MAD THAT THIS HAD HAPPENED TO

HIM AND HAD SCARED HIM OUT OF HIS WITS. HE THEN HITCHED UP HIS DOGTEAM AND WENT BACK TO HIS VILLAGE, DESPITE BEING VERY TIRED, AND ALTHOUGH IT WAS STILL VERY DARK OUTSIDE.

DEAD UNCLE CAUGHT

ONE VERY FINE DAY, THIS VERY MUCH ALIVE WOMAN SOUL HAPPENED TO BE OUT ICE FISHING FOR THE VERY AVAILABLE SMELTS IN HER HOME VILLAGE'S AREA. SHE WAS FISHING THROUGH THE ICE-FISHING HOLE THAT SHE, THE SOUL, HAD MADE, USING HER STONE TOOL FOR CHOPPING UP ICE, WHICH SHE HAD RECENTLY MADE, WITH A WOODEN HANDLE. THIS FISHING SOUL HAD HEARD STORIES THAT THE VERY RECENTLY DEPARTED BODILY DEAD COULD BE CAUGHT AND BE BROUGHT BACK TO LIFE AFTER BEING CAUGHT THROUGH THE ICE-FISHING HOLES BY THEIR LOVED ONES. AND THIS SOUL'S DEARLY BELOVED UNCLE HAD VERY RECENTLY DIED BODILY. THIS SOUL IN QUESTION DID NOT HAVE ANY LUCK IN HER ICE-FISHING DAY. NO SMELT WAS ABOUT TO GIVE UP HIS LIFE FOR HER SO THAT THIS SOUL WOULD HAVE THEM ON HER VERY NEXT COOKOUT. THIS SOUL HAD BEEN FISHING FOR SMELT THROUGH THE ICE-FISHING HOLE THAT SHE HAD CHOPPED OPEN THAT DAY, AND HAD BEEN FISHING FOR FISH THROUGH THE ICE HOLE ALL MORNING AND ALL THROUGH THE AFTERNOON HOURS, WITHOUT SO MUCH AS A NUDGE BY ANY FISH IN HER IMMEDIATE

AREA. NOT EVEN A BITE HAD BEEN FELT BY THIS FISHING SOUL. BUT JUST WHEN THE EVENING HOURS WERE STARTING UP, AND THE SUN WAS IN ITS PROCESS OF SETTING DOWN OVER THE HORIZON, AND HER SURROUNDING AREA WAS QUICKLY BECOMING QUITE DARK, THE LIVING SOUL FINALLY FELT A NUDGE ON HER FISHING LINE, WHICH WAS MADE OUT OF DRIED ANIMAL SKINS CUT QUITE THIN. THIS SOUL THOUGHT TO HERSELF THAT SHE HAD FINALLY CAUGHT A VERY MUCH NEEDED FISH. THE LIVING SOUL THEN VERY SLOWLY STARTED TO PULL UP HER ANIMAL SKIN LINE. AND AS SHE WAS DOING SO, SHE WAS VERY CONFIDENT THAT YES, IT WAS A VERY MUCH LOVED FISH THAT SHE, THE SOUL, HAD FINALLY CAUGHT THAT DAY. WHEN SHE FELT THAT SHE COULD SEE WHAT SHE HAD CAUGHT, AND LOOKED THROUGH HER ICE HOLE, THE SOUL RECOGNIZED THE CAP OF HER MUCH LOVED UNCLE WHO HAD DIED BODILY VERY RECENTLY, ALONG WITH HER VERY MUCH LOVED UNCLE'S BODY UNDERNEATH IT. THE POOR SOUL GOT VERY FRIGHTENED, SO SHE CUT HER SKIN-MADE FISHING LINE WITH HER HANDY STONE KNIFE. THEN, HER UNCLE, WHOM SHE HAD JUST CAUGHT, ONCE AGAIN RETURNED TO BEING A BODILY DEAD MAN RIGHT AFTER SINKING BACK DOWN THROUGH HER FISHING HOLE. SHE, THE FISHING SOUL, THEN HURRIED BACK TO HER HOME VILLAGE AND TOLD ALL SOULS THAT SHE HAPPENED

TO MEET THAT DAY ABOUT WHAT HAD JUST OCCURRED DURING HER SMELT-FISHING MISHAP.

YEAR GONE

THIS OLD LIVING SOUL DECIDED FOR HERSELF ONE DAY THAT SHE WOULD GO DOWN TO THE BEACH AREA OF HER CURRENT HOME VILLAGE. THAT DAY WOULD TURN OUT TO BE REALLY GOOD INDEED FOR THIS VERY OLD SOUL, WHO WAS LIVING OUT HER LAST DAYS. FIRST, SHE GOT HER THINGS THAT SHE KNEW SHE WOULD NEED FOR THAT SOMEWHAT LUCKY DAY. SHE ALSO PREPARED SOME FOOD THAT SHE WOULD DEFINITELY NEED, AND COUNTED ON FOR HER MUCH NEEDED STRENGTH FOR HER RETURN TRIP BACK TO HER CURRENT SMALL VILLAGE. SHE STARTED OFF FROM HER VERY MUCH LIVED-IN DWELLING PLACE QUITE SLOWLY, FOR THE TRUE FACT WAS THAT SHE, THE VERY OLD SOUL, WAS WELL OVER HER GOLDEN YEARS AND WAS INDEED QUITE AGED. THE OLD SOUL HAD PLANNED BEFOREHAND TO GATHER SOME EDIBLE GREENS FROM THE BEACH AREA CLOSE TO HER HOME VILLAGE. SHE KNEW WITHIN HER OLD HEART THAT VERY DAY THAT THE GREENS WERE VERY RIPE AND READY TO BE GATHERED BY ANYONE WHO WANTED TO DO SO. AS THIS VERY OLD SOUL WALKED VERY SLOWLY TO THE BEACH

SITE, SHE CAME TO AN OPENING THAT WAS ON THE SIDE OF THIS ONE SMALL HILL. SHE THOUGHT TO HERSELF THAT THERE MAY BE SOME NEW SOULS THAT HAD VERY RECENTLY MOVED TO HER VILLAGE'S AREA FROM OTHER PARTS OF THE LAND, SO SHE WENT INSIDE THIS VERY STRANGE DWELLING PLACE. AND INSIDE THIS PLACE, THE VERY OLD SOUL SAW TWO PEOPLE JUST GETTING READY TO HAVE THEIR LUNCH, WHICH CONSISTED OF THE TRADITIONAL FOODS THAT SHE HAD ENJOYED IN HER LIFETIME. ONE OF THE TWO PEOPLE INVITED THIS OLD SOUL TO STAY AND EAT THE FOOD THAT THEY WERE ABOUT TO ENJOY WITH THEM. AND THIS OLD SOUL ACCEPTED THEIR OFFERING TO SHARE THEIR FOOD WITH HER. AFTER THIS VERY OLD SOUL HAD EATEN HER FILL, SHE GOT VERY SLEEPY AND SEEMED VERY TIRED IN HER MIND AND BODY. ONE OF THE TWO PEOPLE TOLD HER THAT SHE COULD REST A BIT, IF SHE WANTED TO GAIN SOME OF HER STRENGTH BACK, KNOWING VERY WELL THAT THE OLD SOUL WAS VERY TIRED FROM HER WALK. THE OLD SOUL FELL RIGHT TO SLEEP ON THE COT MADE OUT OF ANIMAL FURS THAT ONE OF THE TWO HAD PLACED ON THE BARE EARTH FLOOR FOR HER VERY MUCH NEEDED REST. WHEN THIS OLD SOUL HAD HER REST AND CAME TO HER SENSES, THE OLD SOUL FOUND HERSELF OUTDOORS. THERE WAS NO DOOR ON THE SIDE OF THAT HILL, AND NO ONE WAS AROUND, SAVE HER.

HER FUR GARMENTS WERE VERY WORN-OUT, VERY ROTTED-OUT, AND TORN UP, ALSO. THEN THIS VERY OLD SOUL REALIZED THAT SHE HAD SOMEHOW BEEN ALIVE AND WELL UNDERGROUND FOR A YEAR, WHICH HAD ONLY SEEMED TO BE A MOMENT IN THIS OLD SOUL'S MIND. LATER, BACK AT HER VILLAGE, ALL THE OTHER SOULS WERE VERY MUCH SURPRISED TO SEE HER ALIVE AND WELL, KNOWING THAT SHE HAD BEEN GONE FOR A VERY LONG PERIOD OF TIME, BUT WERE NO LONGER SURPRISED RIGHT AFTER SHE HAD TOLD THEM HER STORY OF THAT HOLE ON THAT SIDE OF THIS CERTAIN HILL. THEY KNEW THAT THESE STRANGE OCCURRENCES WERE SOMETIMES TOLD ABOUT IN STORIES FROM WAY BACK IN THE TIMES OF THE PAST.

REVENGE FROM BEYOND

A FORMER SOUL, WHO HAPPENED TO BE A WOMAN, DIED BODILY RIGHT AFTER SHE HAD GIVEN BIRTH TO A VERY ADORABLE BABY SOUL. THE VERY MUCH ALIVE RELATIVES OF THIS FORMER SOUL DID NOT UNDER ANY CIRCUMSTANCE WANT TO HAVE ANYTHING TO DO WITH THE BABY SOUL OF THIS ONCE VERY ACTIVE SOUL MOM, WHO WAS NOW BASICALLY VERY DEAD, BODILY. NOR DID THESE VERY EVIL-MINDED SOULS WANT TO RAISE THIS POOR CHILD AS THEIR OWN. SO, THESE SO-CALLED VERY EVIL-MINDED RELATIVES OF THESE TWO VERY UNFORTUNATE SOULS CAME UP WITH AN ANSWER TO THAT SOMEWHAT SEEMINGLY BIG PROBLEM THEY NOW FACED. JUST WHAT DID THEY COME UP WITH TO SOLVE THEIR LITTLE PROBLEM? THEY DECIDED BY THEIR OWN FREE WILL TO DO A VERY EVIL THING TO THAT SMALL SOUL. THEY BURIED THE SMALL HELPLESS SOUL ALONG WITH HIS NOW VERY BODILY DEAD MOM, ALTHOUGH THE SMALL SOUL WAS HEALTHY AND WAS STILL VERY ALIVE. SO THEREFORE, THESE VERY EVIL-MINDED SOULS CARRIED OUT THEIR MISTAKE AND BURIED THE POOR, VERY HELPLESS YOUNG SOUL SO THAT HE WOULD SUFFOCATE

AND THEREFORE DIE. THESE VERY EVIL SOULS THOUGHT TO THEMSELVES THAT THE VERY LITTLE PROBLEM THEY HAD ON THEIR HANDS WAS NOW SOLVED, BUT THIS WAS NOT TO TURN OUT TO THEIR CONSIDERATIONS. FOR THESE VERY EVIL-MINDED AND WRONG-DOING SOULS, WHO WERE STILL VERY MUCH ALIVE AND STILL WERE IN THE PROCESS OF LIVING OUT THEIR NOW SOMEWHAT EASIER DAILY GIFTS OF THEIR DAILY LIVES, GIVEN TO THEM FOR FREE. THAT VERY SAME NIGHT, THE NOW BODILY DEAD WOMAN'S SPIRIT WAS SEEN AND HEARD WALKING AROUND THIS VERY SMALL VILLAGE, WHICH WAS OCCUPIED BY HER STILL LIVING AND VERY ALIVE RELATIVES. THE SPIRIT WAS ASKING, OF NO ONE IN PARTICULAR, WHO HAD DONE THIS VERY EVIL DEED TO HER BABY. BUT THE POOR SPIRIT GOT NO ANSWERS TO HER SIMPLE QUESTION, DUE TO THE FACT THAT NOT ONE OF THESE EVIL-MINDED SOULS WAS ABOUT TO COME FORWARD AND ADMIT HIS OR HER GUILT TO THE SPIRIT OF THAT NOW BODILY DEAD MOTHER. SO WHAT THIS SPIRIT OUT AND ABOUT THAT NIGHT WAS HEARD SAYING, VERY CLEARLY, WAS THAT SOMETHING VERY EVIL WAS TO BEFALL THE UNRESPONSIVE EVIL SOULS THAT WERE STILL ALIVE AND WELL IN THIS SMALL VILLAGE. THIS SPIRIT MOM'S VERY WORDS BECAME VERY TRUE, IN FACT, BECAUSE NOT VERY LONG AFTER THIS VERY BAD INCIDENT HAD TAKEN PLACE IN THIS

SMALL VILLAGE, A WARRIOR GANG OF SOUL KILLERS CHOSE THIS EVIL-DOING SMALL VILLAGE. AS THEIR NEXT TARGET. THEY WERE GOING TO RAID THIS SMALL VILLAGE OF ITS EDIBLE FOODS, KILL OFF ALL THE DOGS THAT WERE USED IN DOGTEAMS, AND, LAST OF ALL, ELIMINATE ALL THOSE GOOD AND EVIL SOULS WHO HAPPENED TO LIVE OUT THEIR FREE DAILY GIFTS OF THEIR LIVES ONCE AND FOR ALL. ALL WERE KILLED OFF BODILY, SAVE ONE SOUL, AS WAS CUSTOM IN THOSE DAYS. ONE SOUL WAS SAVED TO CARRY THE BAD NEWS TO OTHER NEARBY VILLAGES THAT ALL HAD BEEN ELIMINATED BODILY, AND ALL OF THE RICHES TAKEN. SO, THE REVENGE OF THIS FORMER MOTHER WAS INDEED QUITE BAD, FOR THE WRONG AND EVIL THING THAT THESE VILLAGERS HAD DONE TO HER VERY HELPLESS NEWBORN BABY.

KILLER SPIRIT MOM

THESE TWO LIVING SOULS HAPPENED TO HAVE A BIG QUARREL WITH EACH OTHER ONE FATEFUL DAY. THE FIGHT FOR THESE TWO LIVING SOULS, WHO WERE STILL CARRYING OUT THEIR FREE GIFT OF DAILY LIFE, WENT OUT OF CONTROL QUITE QUICKLY. THE MUCH STONGER MAN KILLED THE OTHER GUY AFTER A MUCH MISMATCHED FIGHT. HE ACCIDENTLY BROKE THE OTHER POOR SOUL'S NECK. WHEN HE REALIZED JUST WHAT HAD HAPPENED, THE STRONGER LIVING SOUL PANICKED AND NOW WOULD BE LABELED A KILLER IF HIS FELLOW MAN SOULS FOUND OUT WHAT HE HAD JUST COMMITTED. SO, THIS MAN VERY HURRIEDLY AND QUITE HASITLY BURIED THE OTHER UNFORTUNATE FORMER GUY, AFTER DIGGING A SHALLOW GRAVE FOR HIM OUT IN THE WILDERNESS. AFTER HE HAD GONE BACK TO HIS SMALL HOME VILLAGE, THE RELATIVES OF THIS SOUL, WHO WAS ONCE AMONG THE VERY ALIVE, INQUIRED AND ASKED THIS KILLER IF HE HAD SEEN THEIR VERY MUCH LOVED RELATIVE ANYWHERE. BUT THIS MAN WAS SOMEWHAT CAPABLE OF DOING SOME WORTHLESS LYING, AND HE DID JUST THAT. HE TOLD THEM, LOOKING QUITE INNOCENT,

THAT HE HAD NOT SEEN THIS FORMER BODILY ALIVE SOUL. HE ALSO STATED THAT HE DID NOT KNOW OF HIS WHEREABOUTS. BUT HE DID KNOW, IN HIS MIND AND SOUL, THAT HE HAD JUST KILLED THAT POOR GUY. THAT NIGHT, THIS KILLER WAS GETTING HIMSELF READY TO SLEEP OFF HIS GUILTY MIND, BUT HE KEPT HEARING SOMETHING OUTSIDE HIS MUD DWELLING'S WINDOW. SO, THIS SOUL DECIDED THAT HE WOULD INVESTIGATE THE SOURCE OF THAT LITTLE DISTURBANCE. HE WAS NOW IN TUNE, TOO. AS THIS SOUL LOOKED OUT HIS WINDOW, HE SAW THE FACE OF HIS ONCE VERY BODILY ALIVE MOTHER, POINTING HER FINGER AT HIM. THIS, OF COURSE, MADE THE STRONG SOUL FEEL QUITE OVERCOME WITH GUILT. HE ALSO FELT VERY ASHAMED OF WHAT HE HAD COMMITTED THAT FATEFUL DAY. AFTER THIS VERY UNUSUAL SIGHTING OF HIS DEAD MOM POINTING HER FINGER AT HIM, AS IF TO LET HIM KNOW THAT HE WAS INDEED GUILTY OF THAT VERY BAD INCIDENT, THE STONG SOUL IMMEDIATELY WENT OVER TO THE DEAD MAN'S RELATIVES' HOUSE AND CONFESSED TO THEM WHAT HE HAD VERY RECENTLY DONE TO THEIR NOW BODILY DEAD RELATIVE. THE NEXT DAY, SOME LOCAL VILLAGERS WENT OUT TO THE AREA WHERE THE DEAD MAN WAS BURIED IN A SHALLOW GRAVE, TO RETRIEVE HIS DEAD BODY SO THAT THEY COULD AT LEAST GIVE HIM A DECENT BURIAL AT THE VILLAGE GRAVESITE. WHAT HAPPENED TO THIS KILLER

AFTERWARDS WAS THAT HE WAS KICKED OUT OF THIS VILLAGE AND WAS BANNED FROM EVER RETURNING AGAIN. THANKS VERY MUCH TO THIS KILLER'S MOM'S SPIRIT SOUL, THIS VERY GUILTY SOUL GOT WHAT HE DESERVED FOR SOMETHING VERY BAD, INDEED, WHICH HE HAD COMMITTED. IT MAY HAVE BEEN ACCIDENTALLY CARRIED OUT, FOR THAT QUARREL AMONG THOSE TWO MEN, GOT OUT OF CONTROL, AND COST THAT OTHER MAN HIS ONLY GIFT OF LIFE THAT HE CARRIED OUT ON A DAILY BASIS IN THAT SMALL VILLAGE. BUT HE COULD NO LONGER DO SO, FOR HE WAS NOW VERY MUCH BODILY DEAD, DUE TO GETTING INTO A FIGHT WITH HIS FELLOW MAN, WHO WAS NOW BANNED FROM THE VILLAGE THAT BOTH OF THEM ONCE LIVED IN.

SNATCHED

THESE TWO VERY YOUNG SOULS, WHO
APPEARED IN OUR WORLD, WHICH IS VERY
GOOD INDEED, AS BABIES AWHILE BACK,
HAPPENED TO BE CARRYING OUT THEIR DAILY
GIFTS OF THEIR SOMEWHAT FUN-FILLED DAILY
YOUNG LIVES IN THIS VERY SMALL VILLAGE.
ONE FATE-CONTROLLED NIGHT, THESE TWO
YOUNG SOULS WERE PLAYING SOME FUN
GAMES THAT THEY WANTED TO CARRY OUT
THAT VERY SAME EVENING. ON THAT NIGHT IN
QUESTION, THAT SMALL VILLAGE WAS QUITE
COLD OUTSIDE, BUT THESE TWO SMALL SOULS
DID THEIR PLAYING NONETHELESS. ONCE IN A
WHILE, THE TWO WHISTLED QUITE LOUDLY
DURING THIS PLAYTIME HOUR, FOR THESE
TWO DID NOT KNOW EVERYTHING GOING ON
THIS WORLD OF OURS. THE TWO OF THEM
HAPPENED TO BE DOING THEIR BUSINESS OF
WHISTLING AT THE VERY BRIGHT NORTHERN
LIGHTS, WHICH WERE DOING THEIR THING UP
ABOVE, IN THE SKY, DURING THAT VERY SAME
STAR-FILLED NIGHT WITH A VERY CLEAR
SKY--NOT TO MENTION, THESE LIGHTS WERE
ALSO CHANGING COLORS WHILE DOING
THEIR THING. THE TWO VERY YOUNG SOULS
THEREFORE KEPT WHISTLING LOUDLY AT

THOSE SORT OF COOL-LOOKING, BRIGHT NORTHERN LIGHTS. AS THESE TWO YOUNG SOULS WERE GOING ABOUT THEIR BUSINESS AT THAT MOMENT IN TIME, THE BRIGHT LIGHTS SEEMED TO BE GETTING CLOSER AND CLOSED TO THESE YOUNG BOYS AND THEIR WHISTLING AREA. AND THE LIGHTS SOMEHOW SEEMED BRIGHTER, WHEN THEY GOT TOO CLOSE TO THE YOUNG SOULS FOR THEIR LIKING. ONE OF THOSE TWO YOUNG INDIVIDUALS RAN IN ONE OF THE HOUSES IN THEIR SMALL VILLAGE, LEAVING HIS PLAYMATE BUDDY TO DEAL WITH THEM AS HE WISHED. AFTER BEING IN THAT LOCAL HOME FOR QUITE A SPELL, THIS OTHER YOUNG SOUL LEFT THAT HOME THAT HE HAD RUN IN ABOUT A HALF AN HOUR OR SO AGO, TO SEE IF HIS BUDDY WAS STILL OUT AND ABOUT IN THEIR FORMER PLAYTIME AREA. BUT FOR SOME VERY ODD REASON, HE COULD NOT LOCATE HIS BUDDY. SO, HE WENT BACK TO HIS PARENTS' HOME, THINKING TO HIMSELF THAT THE OT HER YOUNG SOUL HAD LEFT HIM AND HAD GONE HOME. LATER THAT EVENING, WHEN THE NOW MISSING YOUNG SOUL'S PARENTS ASKED THIS YOUNG BOY ABOUT THEIR NOW MISSING SON, THE YOUNG BOY TOLD THE MISSING YOUNG SOUL'S MOM AND DAD THE WHOLE STORY--THAT THE TWO OF THEM HAD BEEN WHISTLING AT THE NORTHERN LIGHTS, AND HE, THE YOUNG SOUL, RAN IN THIS HOUSE, LEAVING THEIR NOW MISSING SON OUTSIDE. HE ALSO TOLD

THEM THAT WHEN HE HAD LEFT THAT HOME IN QUESTION, THEIR MISSING SON WAS NOWHERE IN THE PLAYING AREA THAT THE TWO OF THEM HAD BEEN IN. THAT WAS WHEN EVERY ONE OF THE GROWNUPS KNEW AND ALSO REALIZED THE WHOLE TRUTH, THAT THE NOW LOST YOUNG SOUL WAS TAKEN BY THOSE BRIGHT NORTHERN LIGHTS. SO THE LOST BOY'S PARENTS THEREFORE LET IT BE, AND DID NOT ASK ANYMORE QUESTIONS, KNOWING AT THAT VERY MOMENT THAT THEIR NOW MISSING SON WOULD NEVER RETURN TO THEM, BUT WOULD PLAY HIS MUCH LOVED GAMES AMONG THE NORTHEN LIGHTS EACH AND EVERY NIGHT. LATER ON, AFTER THIS LITTLE INCIDENT, THE OTHER SMALL SOUL RAN HOME TO HIS PARENTS' HOME WHENEVER HE SPOTTED THOSE LIGHTS IN THE NORTHERN SKY, DOING THEIR THING. HE KNEW IN HIS VERY YOUNG MIND THAT HIS FRIEND HAD BEEN SNATCHED AND TAKEN AWAY FROM HIM BY THE NORTHERN LIGHTS NOT VERY LONG AGO IN HIS YOUNG PAST.

DARKMAN'S CURSE

ONCE THERE WAS A LIVING SOUL, WHO DID HAPPENED TO BE A WOMAN, AND THIS YOUNG LADY LIVED ALL BY HERSELF IN THIS VERY SMALL VILLAGE, IN A HOUSE THAT SHE CLAIMED TO OWN HERSELF. ONE DAY THAT WAS A BAD DAY FOR HER, AS SHE WAS CARRYING OUT HER FREE DAILY GIFT OF HER ONGOING DAILY EXISTENCE HERE ON OUR HOME, THE EARTH, SHE, THE POOR SOUL LIVING ALONE HAPPENED TO MAKE THE LOCAL DARKNESS-LOVING SOUL OF HER VILLAGE SOMEHOW MAD ENOUGH TO PUT A CURSE ON HER. THIS NOW VERY MAD, DARKNESS-LOVING SOUL, WHO WAS ALSO KNOWN ALL AROUND FOR BEING A BAD SHAMAN, TOLD THIS LADY THAT FROM THAT VERY FATEFUL DAY ON, HER DAILY GIFT OF LIFE WOULD VERY WELL BE QUITE DIFFERENT FROM THE ONE SHE CURRENTLY KNEW FROM HER SOMEWHAT GOOD PAST. THIS BAD, EVIL-KNOWING AND DARKNESS-LOVING SOUL LET IT BE KNOWN TO THIS LADY THAT HE WAS GOING TO SUMMON AND THEREFORE SEND A VERY EVIL DEMON TO LIVE AT HER CURRENT RESIDENCE. THE DEMON WOULD MAKE IT VERY MISERABLE FOR HER TO CARRY OUT HER DAILY EXISTENCE HERE

ON EARTH, FOR HER AND HER ALONE, FOR
THAT MATTER. BUT THIS SOMEWHAT HARD-
HEADED AND SELF-DIRECTED LADY WAS IN
NO MOOD TO BELIEVE THE WORDS THAT HAD
JUST BEEN HEARD BY HER OWN EARS, WHICH
SHE HAD HEARD COMING FROM THE MOUTH
OF THAT DARKNESS-LOVING MAN. SO, SHE
MADE SOME UNUSUAL FACES AT THAT BAD
SHAMAN THAT WAS FACING HER. ALSO, A
LOT OF NAME-CALLING WAS CARRIED OUT
BY THIS LADY, WHO WAS NOW A VERY MAD
SELF-LOVING LADY SOUL, INDEED. MUCH TO
HER DISMAY, SHE LATER FOUND OUT THAT
SOMETIMES EVEN THE BAD WERE VERY
CAPABLE OF TELLING THE TRUTH, ALL IN ALL,
IF IT HAS TO BE THAT THE TRUTH WAS FOR A
VERY BAD CAUSE TOWARDS ANOTHER WHO
WAS NOT LIKED BY THE BAD SOUL. WHEN
THIS LADY HAPPENED TO REACH HER HOUSE
THAT EVENING, AND THEREFORE WENT INSIDE
HER HOUSE, THE VERY UNUSUAL THING WAS
THAT HER HOME, SWEET HOME, WAS, FOR
SOME REASON NOT KNOWN TO HER AT THAT
VERY MOMENT, WAS VERY DEATHLY COLD
INSIDE. SO SHE FIRED UP HER STOVE FULL
BLAST, YET HER PLACE REMAINED COLD, NO
MATTER WHAT THIS LADY SOUL TRIED TO DO.
AND THE OTHER UNUSUAL THING WAS THAT
THINGS LIKE HER CUPS AND HER DISHES
WOULD LEVITATE ON THEIR OWN, AND MOVE
ABOUT HER PLACE BY THEMSELVES, OR SO IT
SEEMED. THEN SHE REMEMBERED THAT SHE

HAD BEEN HEXED THAT VERY SAME DAY, BY THAT BAD SOUL WHO WAS VERY MUCH INTO DARKNESS AND LIVED ONLY FOR EVIL. THAT SOUL TOLD THIS WOMAN THAT HE WOULD SEND AN EVIL DEMON TO LIVE WITH HER AT HER PLACE. AFTER HE HAD USED HIS EVIL-SUMMONING MAGIC POWERS TO DO SO, ALL OF THESE ONGOING, VERY ODD OCCURRENCES WENT ON FOR A COUPLE OF DAYS, UNTIL THIS LADY GOT QUITE FED UP WITH ALL THE EVIL THINGS NOW TAKING PLACE IN HER HOME. SO ONE DAY, SHE SUMMONED A VERY ALIVE PRIEST TO COME TO HER PLACE AND REMOVE THE CURRENT HEX, WHICH THE VERY BAD SHAMAN HAD PLACED ON HER. WHEN THE PRIEST CAME TO HER HOUSE, WHAT THESE TWO SOULS HEARD WAS A VERY EVIL-SOUNDING VOICE TELLING THE PRIEST TO GET OUT OF THE HOUSE. BUT THE GOOD SOUL DAIS AND PRAYED SOME DEMON-REMOVAL RITES. AT THAT VERY MOMENT, THESE TWO SOULS FELT A VERY QUICKLY MOVING COLD AIR AND HEARD THE EVIL DEMON SCREAM VERY LOUDLY AS HE LEFT THIS LADY SOUL'S HOUSE. THINGS GOT BACK TO NORMAL FOR THIS LADY AFTERWARDS, AND NO MORE UNUSUAL HAPPENINGS TOOK PLACE RIGHT AFTER HER HOME WAS BLESSED BY A MAN OF GOD.

SAVED FROM CERTAIN DEATH

ONE VERY FATEFUL DAY, A GROUP OF WARRIOR SOULS CAME TO THIS ONE SMALL VILLAGE, TO RAID IT OF ITS THINGS TO EAT, WHICH HAD BEEN GATHERED FOR THE QUICKLY APPROACHING WINTER MONTHS. THE EVIL KILLERS WENT ABOUT THEIR TASK OF COLD-BLOODED MURDER, WITHOUT SHOWING ANY MERCY WHATSOEVER FOR THESE POOR VILLAGE-LIVING SOULS WHO WERE VERY MUCH INTO THEIR SURIVAL RESPONSIBILITIES EACH AND EVERY DAY. BUT THIS ONE SOUL, WHO HAPPENED TO BE A MAN, RAN RIGHT OFF INTO THE VERY UNFORGIVING WILDERNESS, WITH SOME OF THE MURDERING SOULS RUNNING AFTER HIM WITH ONLY THE THOUGHT OF ENDING THIS POOR SOUL'S ONLY GIFT OF HIS DAILY LIFE. THEY WERE RUNNING RIGHT BEHIND HIM. BUT THIS MAN WHO WAS RUNNING AWAY MAN SO THAT HE COULD AT LEAST LIVE ANOTHER DAY, SOON DID GET A LITTLE TOO WORN OUT TO CONTINUE OR CARRY ON RUNNING AWAY FROM THOSE PEOPLE-KILLERS. SO WHAT HE DID WAS THIS: HE DECIDED THAT HE WOULD SURRENDER HIS ONLY LIFE TO THOSE BLOODTHIRSTY LIFE-ENDERS, WHO WERE COMING UP TOO QUICKLY

FOR HIS LIKING, AND WERE NOW VERY CLOSE, RIGHT BEHIND HIM. AND WHEN THIS RUNNING SOUL CAME TO THIS ONE HILL, HE WENT OVER THE HILL. WHAT HE DID SEE ON THE OTHER SIDE OF THAT HILL? HE SAW A MAN STANDING BY AN OPENING IN THE SIDE OF THAT HILL. WHAT THAT MAN SAID TO THE RUNNING SOUL WAS THIS: "QUICK, COME INTO MY HOME WITH ME. I WILL HIDE YOU FROM YOUR ONCOMING ENEMIES." THIS RUNNING MAN LISTENED TO THAT OTHER MAN, WHO THEN TOLD HIM THAT HE WOULD BE SAFE ONLY IF HE WOULD COME INSIDE HIS HOME WITH HIM. SO HE, THE RUNNING SOUL, DID GO INSIDE THAT OTHER MAN'S HOME WITHOUT ASKING TOO MANY QUESTIONS, KNOWING THAT THE ENEMY WARRIORS WOULD KILL HIM IF HE DID NOT DO SO. THE INSIDE OF THAT OTHER MAN'S HOME WAS LIT UP WITH A SEAL OIL LAMP, AS HE NOTICED. THIS STRANGER THEN TOLD HIM TO SIT DOWN ON A SEAT MADE OUT OF SOME FURS THAT HAD BEEN PLACED ON THE DIRT FLOOR. THE STRANGER TOLD HIM THAT HE WAS GOING TO FEED HIM, AND LET HIM GO AFTERWARDS. AFTER ALL HAD BEEN SAID AND DONE, WHAT THAT STRANGER SAID TO HIM REALLY SURPISED HIM. WHAT HE SAID TO HIM WAS THIS: "BEFORE YOU CAN LEAVE MY PLACE, I WILL LET YOU CHOOSE ONE OF THESE THREE DOORS." WHAT THIS RUNNING SOUL SAW WERE THE THREE DOORS THAT THIS STRANGER WAS TALKING ABOUT. THE

DOORS WERE ON THE INSIDE AREA OF HIS HOME. THEN, HE TOLD HIM THAT ONE DOOR WOULD TAKE HIM TO A VERY BEATIFUL, GOOD PLACE; ONE OF THE DOORS WOULD TAKE HIM TO A VERY, VERY BAD PLACE; AND IF HE HAPPENED TO CHOOSE THE RIGHT DOOR, HE WOULD FIND HIMSELF BACK AT HIS VILLAGE'S AREA. THIS RUNNING SOUL THEN PLEADED WITH THAT STRANGER TO ALLOW HIM TO STAY A LITTLE LONGER, BECAUSE THE FACT WAS THAT IT SEEMED TO HIM THAT HE HAD BEEN IN THIS STRANGER'S HOME FOR ONLY AN HOUR OR SO. BUT THE OTHER MAN REASSURED AND PROMISED HIM THAT HIS LIFE WOULD NOT END THAT DAY. SO DESPITE NOT WANTING TO GO OUT, HE DID CHOOSE THE MIDDLE DOOR, AND THEN WENT OUT. SURE ENOUGH, HE HAD CHOSEN THE RIGHT DOOR, WHICH LED BACK TO THE AREA HE HAD ONCE LIVED IN, MINUS ITS FORMER BODILY ALIVE, BUT NOW DEAD AND GONE SOULS. BUT WHEN HE CAME TO HIS SENSES, HE FOUND THAT HIS GARMENTS HAD BEEN EATEN UP BY WORMS AND WERE ROTTED-OUT AND USELESS. HE REALIZED THEN THAT HE HAD BEEN WITH THAT STRANGER FOR ABOUT A YEAR OR SO, WHICH IN HIS MIND HAD LASTED FOR ONLY AN HOUR. HIS LIFE HAD BEEN SAVED FOR SOME REASON THAT HE COULD NOT POSSIBLY SOLVE BY HIMSELF.

DID NOT WORK OUT

A VERY MUCH LOVED SOUL HAD JUST DIED BODILY, VERY RECENTLY, AND THE FAMILY OF THIS ONCE BODILY ALIVE SOUL, WHICH WAS LEFT BEHIND, CHOSE TO MAKE A DEAL WITH THE LOCAL VILLAGE'S SOMEWHAT POWERFUL SHAMAN. THEY WANTED THIS FORMERLY FULL-OF-LIFE, MUCH LOVED MAN BACK AMONG THE LIVING ONCE AGAIN. BUT THAT SOMEWHAT POWERFUL LIVING SOUL DID NOT TELL THEM, FOR REASONS KNOWN ONLY TO HIMSELF, THAT HE COULD ONLY BE BROUGHT BACK IN HIS BODILY DEAD FORM. HE MADE THEM PAY HIM WITH FOOD THAT HE COULD LIVE OFF DURING HIS LIFE HERE ON EARTH, DOING HIS WORK, WHICH INVOLVED MANY THINGS THAT WOULD EITHER HELP OR BREAK THE ONGOING LIVES OF HIS FELLOW VILLAGERS. HE KNEW THAT THE SHORT END OF THEIR WANT WAS ALSO DANGEROUS WORK, WHICH WOULD INVOLVE HELP FROM THE VERY EVIL DARK SIDE OF THE UNDERWORLD. AFTER DOING THE SOMEWHAT HEAVY MAGICAL BUSINESS, KNOWN ONLY TO THIS SHAMAN SOUL INVOLVED IN THIS VERY RISKY SITUATION OF BRINGING BACK LIFE, HE TOLD THESE LOVING OR HATEFUL SOULS

THAT THEY WOULD HAVE THEIR CHANCE TO
SEE THEIR DEARLY DEPARTED THAT VERY
SAME NIGHT. BUT HE HAD BEEN PLACED
UNDERGROUND ALREADY. THEY TOLD THE
SHAMAN SO, BUT THE SHAMAN TOLD THESE
SOULS NOT TO WORRY ABOUT ANYTHING.
SO THESE LIVING SOULS THEREFORE WENT
HOME TO WAIT FOR THEIR DEARLY DEPARTED
LOVED ONE'S RETURN FROM AMONG THE
LIFELESS. THAT VERY SAME NIGHT, AS THESE
SOULS WAITED HOPEFULLY FOR THEIR STILL
VERY DEAD RELATIVE'S RETURN, THESE LIVING
SOULS HEARD A VERY LOUD CRACK OUTSIDE
THEIR HOUSE. THEN, A LOUD KNOCK WAS
HEARD BY ALL, COMING FROM THE CORNER
OF THEIR HOUSE. KNOWING TRUTHFULLY
WITHIN THEIR VERY SOPHISTICATED HEARTS
THAT THEIR VERY MUCH LOVED RELATIVE HAD
INDEED RETURNED TO THEM FROM DEATH,
THEY THEREFORE RAN OUT TO MEET THEIR
VERY DEAD LOVED ONE. BUT AS SOON AS
ONE OF THEM GAVE HIM A HUG, HE REALIZED
THAT HE WAS HUGGING THE STILL VERY
DEAD BODY OF THEIR LOVED ONE, WHICH WAS
NOW FROZEN SOLID AND STIFF FROM BEING
BURIED BENEATH THE FROZEN GROUND. ALL
OF THE OTHER SOULS RAN BACK INSIDE, SAVE
THE HUGGER, WHO WAS STILL WITH THE
VERY FROZEN BODY OF THEIR MUCH LOVED,
FORMERLY BODILY ALIVE RELATIVE. SO THIS
SOUL IN QUESTION DECIDED THAT HE WOULD
RETURN THIS VERY DEAD AND NOW ALSO

FROZEN RELATIVE OF THEIRS BACK TO HIS GRAVE. SO HE STARTED TO PUSH, BUT IT WAS VERY SLOW WORK, BECAUSE WHENEVER THIS PUSHING SOUL PUSHED FORWARD A LITTLE TOO HARD, THE CORPSE WOULD MOVE BACKWARDS. SO PUSHING HIM SLOWLY TOOK A LONG TIME, AND WHEN HE HAD FINALLY REACHED HIS BURIAL GRAVESITE, THIS SOUL IN QUESTION HAD TO PUSH DOWNWARD INTO THE FROZEN GROUND, ALSO VERY SLOWLY. FOR EACH TIME THE DOWNWARD PUSH WAS FORCED A LITTLE TOO HARD, THE VERY MUCH DEAD AND FROZEN BODY WOULD POP BACK UP AGAIN. BUT THIS PUSHING SOUL FINALLY FINISHED THE VERY DREADFUL WORK OF RETURNING THAT DEAD BODY TO ITS GRAVE. AFTER A VERY COLD, DARK, LONG NIGHT OF RETURNING THE DEAD BACK TO DEATH, HE RETURNED HOME SAFELY, VERY TIRED AND, NOT TO MENTION, ALSO VERY COLD FROM BEING OUTDOORS FOR QUITE A SPELL.

DEMON-CONTROLLED ATTIC CLAW

A VERY MUCH ALIVE MAN WAS LYING AROUND ON THE TOP OF HIS MUCH USED BED VERY LATE ONE EVENING. AT THAT PARTICULAR TIME AND PLACE, AS HE WAS NOW VERY RELAXED AND THEREFORE FEELING NO PAIN, THE LAID-UP SOUL HEARD SOMETHING MAKING SOME NOISE COMING FROM HIS HOME'S ATTIC AREA. THEN THIS SOMETHING, WHICH THIS SOUL THAT WAS VERY MUCH ALIVE REALLY HEARD, WAS ALSO HEARD MOVING TOWARDS THE OPENING OF HIS ATTIC. IN THIS CASE, THE OPENING HAPPENED TO BE COVERED UP WITH A SOMEWHAT BIG BOARD OF WOOD, WHOSE PURPOSE WAS TO COVER UP THE OPENING. THE VERY MUCH ALIVE SOUL IN QUESTION BECAME A LITTLE ALARMED BY THIS UNKNOWN NOISE THAT WAS NOW COMING DIRECTLY FROM HIS HOME'S ATTIC. AND HE BECAME WIDE AWAKE RIGHT THEN AND THERE. SO THIS SOUL THOUGHT TO HIMSELF THAT HE WOULD CHECK OUT THE SOUCE OF THAT NOISE, WHICH HE WAS NOW HEARING FROM HIS ATTIC. AFTER THE SOUL HAD GOTTEN A CHAIR SO THAT HE COULD REACH HIS ATTIC'S COVERED UP OPENING, HE CLIMBED ON TOP OF THAT CHAIR AND REACHED

UP TO UNCOVER HIS HOME'S ATTIC. AFTER HE HAD DONE SO, AND WAS LOOKING AROUND HIS ATTIC, WITH ONLY HIS HEAD AND UP TO HIS NECK REVEALED, THE VERY ALIVE SOUL SAW SOMETHING THAT HAD NOT EVER IN HIS VERY SANE MIND BEEN SEEN BEFORE. WHAT WAS SEEN BY THIS ATTIC-CHECKING SOUL WAS AN EVIL, EVIL-LOOKING CLAW HAND. WITHOUT A SINGLE DOUBT, IT WAS VERY MUCH INDEED CONTROLLED BY THE VERY INVISIBLE FOUL-ODORED DEMONS, WHO WERE FULL OF ONLY VERY HARMFUL INTENTS. THAT WAS WHEN THIS SOUL IN QUESTION FROZE IN PLACE, AND ALL HIS FORMER MOVING AROUND BUSINESS STOPPED WORKING. AFTER THE EVIL CLAWED HAND HAD REACHED THIS VERY UNMOVING MAN, IT GOT A HOLD OF HIS NECK, WHICH WAS EXPOSED VERY MUCH. IT STARTED TO SQUEEZE THIS POOR SOUL'S NECK VERY SLOWLY, ALL THE WHILE LIFTING HIM UP VERY SLOWLY TO THE QUITE DARK AND COLD ATTIC OF THIS POOR, POOR SOUL'S HOME. THIS POOR SOUL WAS NOW SUSPENDED IN OPEN AIR, GOING UP TO HIS ATTIC AGAINST HIS WILL. HE WAS VERY QUICKLY RUNNING OUT OF THE VERY PRECIOUS AIR THAT HE DEPENDED ON TO CARRY OUT HIS VERY PRECIOUS AND FREE DAILY LIFE. JUST THEN AND THERE, AT THAT VERY BAD MOMENT THAT THIS POOR SOUL WAS NOW EXPERIENCING, HIS MOUTH DROOLED SOME SALIVA ONTO THAT CLAWED-UP EVIL HAND. THEN, AS SOON AS THIS SOUL

HAD HIS DROOL ON THAT VERY STRANGE AND VERY SCARY THING, THIS SOUL, NOW SUSPENDED IN THE AIR, HEARD A VERY LOUD, EAR-PIERCING SCREAM COMING FROM THE FOUL-ODORED CLAW HAND. THEN THE CLAW LET GO OF THIS MAN'S NECK, STEAMING UP FOUL-ODORED AIR ALL THE WHILE. THEN VERY QUICKLY MOVING FOOTSTEPS WERE HEARD BY THIS POOR, POOR SOUL. AS HE FELL DOWN AND LANDED ON THE FLOOR OF HIS HOME, THIS VERY ALIVE SOUL REALIZED. THAT HIS DROOLED-OUT SALIVA HAD WON THE BATTLE AGAINST THAT HAIRY, EVIL, DEMON-CONTROLLED CLAW HAND THAT HAD ALMOST (BUT HAD NOT HAD) ITS CHANCE TO TAKE THIS POOR SOUL INTO THE VERY UNKNOWN WORLD. THE UNKNOWN WORLD IS VERY MUCH HIDDEN, SO THAT THE EXTENT OF ITS WICKEDNESS COULD BE KEPT HIDDEN, SO THAT MOST OF THE SOULS WOULD NOT EVEN KNOW THAT THE BADNESS OF IT IS MUCH WORSE THAN MOST HAD THOUGHT BEFORE.

SOMETHING VERY BRIGHT

A VERY SMALL BABY HAD RECENTLY DIED BODILY IN THIS VERY SMALL COMMUNITY, AND THAT VERY SMALL AND VERY YOUNG BABY HAD BEEN ONE OF THE UNFORTUNATE ONES TO APPEAR IN OUR VERY GOOD WORLD, SOMETIMES KNOWN BY EVERY LIVING SOUL AS THE EARTH, WHICH IS STILL AROUND. THAT SMALL DEAD CHILD IN QUESTION HAD BEEN BORN WITH SOME SORT OF SICKNESS THAT NO SOUL ALIVE WAS QUITE ABLE TO DIAGNOSE AND NO ONE COULD FIND ANY AVAILABLE CURE FOR THAT SMALL DEAD CHILD'S SICKNESS. AND RESIDENTS OF THIS SAID SMALL DWELLING PLACE, WHO WERE VERY ALIVE AND HAD BEEN LEFT BEHIND, HAD PLACED THE NOW LIFELESS BODY OF THE SMALL BABY IN THEIR LOCAL CHURCH, AND NOW WERE IN THE PROCESS OF CARRYING OUT THEIR LAST GOODBYES, WHICH WOULD LAST ABOUT THREE DAYS OR SO. ALL OF THE LIVING AND VERY MUCH ALIVE SOULS WERE DOING THEIR VISITATIONS FOR THAT SMALL LIFELESS BABY DURING THE COURSE OF THAT THREE-DAY PERIOD GIVEN TO THEM TO CARRY OUT THEIR VISITATION. BUT THESE TWO EVIL-MINDED BAD LIVING SOULS WERE VERY MUCH

NOT INTO ANY DAYTIME VISITATIONS FOR THAT SMALL CHILD, DUE TO THEIR CONTINUATION OF THEIR LIVES, IN WHICH THEY HAD CHOSEN THE WRONG PATHWAY, WHICH THEY WERE STILL VERY MUCH INTO, AND WERE STILL AT IT DAILY. SO WHAT THESE TWO SO-LABELED BAD BOYS DID THAT SAME LATE EVENING WAS THAT ONE OF THE TWO TOLD HIS OTHER BAD BUDDY THAT HE WANTED TO SAY HIS LAST GOOD BYES TO THAT VERY SMALL BODILY DEAD BABY IN QUESTION. SO HE SET OUT TO THAT LOCAL CHURCH'S AREA, THINKING TO HIMSELF ALL SORTS OF STUFF AND WHATNOT. AS THIS SO-CALLED EVIL-LOVING SOUL WAS WALKING ALONG TO THAT CHURCH'S AREA, HE LOOKED AT THAT CHURCH. WHAT THIS BAD SOUL SAW ON THE FRONT STEPS OF THAT BUILDING WAS A VERY BRIGHT FORM OF A HUMAN, STANDING ON THE STEPS. THIS BAD SOUL THEN GOT QUITE SCARED, KNOWING VERY MUCH WITHIN HIS VERY OWN HEART THAT HE WAS A BAD MAN. SO, HE PRETENDED THAT NOTHING WAS SEEN BY HIM. ALSO, HE PLAYED PASSING UP THE CHURCH, AS IF HE HAD NOT GONE OUT VERY LATE THAT EVENING TO SAY HIS LAST GOODBYES TO THAT SMALL BODILY DEAD CHILD. WHEN HE HAD COME BACK SO EARLY, THE OTHER LIVING BAD SOUL ASKED HIM WHY HE WAS BACK SO SOON FROM HIS TRIP TO SEE THAT BODILY DEAD BABY. SO THE OTHER BAD SOUL TOLD ALL THAT WAS SEEN BY HIM AS HE WAS

APPROCHING THAT CHURCH ON THAT SAME LATE EVENING. ALSO, THESE TWO SOMEWHAT BAD SOULS ON LIFE'S BAD ROAD DID NOT ATTEND THE SMALL BODILY DEAD BABY'S FUNERAL, THINKING THAT THE VERY BRIGHT HUMAN FORM OF LIGHT WAS A VERY BAD OMEN FOR JUST THE TWO OF THEM. AND NO, THEY DID NOT FIND OUT WHAT THAT BRIGHTLY LIT HUMAN FORM WAS, WHICH WAS SEEN BY ONE OF THESE TWO BAD SOULS. THEY THEREFORE DID TRY TO FIND OUT WHAT IT WAS, BELIEVING IN THEIR WRONG-THINKING MINDS THAT SOMEONE WAS TRYING TO PUT A HEX ON THEIR ONGOING DAILY GIFTS OF THEIR LIVES THAT THEY STILL HAPPENED TO CARRY OUT, DOING MANY WRONGS. THESE WILL EVENTUALLY TAKE THEM TO THE WRONG SPOT, SOMEDAY SOONER THAN THEY THINK, AND BEFORE THEY KNOW WHAT IS RIGHT AND WHAT IS NOT RIGHT, BEFORE TOO LONG.

RESTORED YOUTH WITH MAGIC POWERS

AN OLD SOUL, WHO HAPPENED TO BE AN OLD LADY, WAS OUT IN THE WOODED WILDERNESS ONE VERY GOOD DAY, ON HER WAY BACK TO HER MUD-BUILT DWELLING PLACE. AT THAT PARTICULAR TIME AND PLACE, THIS INDIVIDUAL LIVING OLD SOUL DID HAVE A CANE MADE OUT OF DRIFTWOOD, WHICH HAD BEEN SHAPED AND FORMED BY ONE OF THE YOUNG SOULS FROM HER VERY SMALL HOME VILLAGE. SHE THEREFORE USED IT TO HELP HER STAND UPRIGHT AND IT DID, IN FACT, KEEP HER FROM FALLING DOWN TO THE GROUND, MANY TIMES. ALSO, SHE USED HER CANE AS A CLUB, OCCASIONALLY, WHENEVER SOMETHING NEEDED TO BE CLUBBED BY HER AND HER ALONE, FOR THAT MATTER. AS THIS OLD SOUL DID HER MUCH NEEDED WALK, SHE VERY SOON GOT TIRED OUT, AND THEREFORE WAS IN NEED OF RESTING HER OLD BODY A BIT BEFORE SHE CONTINUED ON THE LAST LEG OF HER WALK BACK TO HER MUD-BUILT HOME. AS THIS SOMEWHAT OLD SOUL WAS ON HER RESTING SPOT, SHE SPOTTED WITH THE USE OF HER SOMEWHAT CLEARLY-SEEING OLD EYES SOMETHING VERY DIFFERENT THAN ANYTHING SHE HAD EVER SEEN BEFORE IN

HER PAST. WHAT THIS OLD SOUL SAW WAS SOME CUTE-LOOKING LITTLE FAIRY GIRLS, FLYING IN THE AIR, PLAYING SOME GAMES THAT WERE VERY GOOD FOR THEM AND THEIR SELF-WORTH. ALSO, WHAT WAS NOTED BY THIS OLD SOUL WAS THAT THE FAIRY GIRLS WERE HAPPY AND LAUGHING ABOUT SOMETHING, THOUGHT THE OLD SOUL DID NOT KNOW WHAT THEY WERE LAUGHING ABOUT. THE OLD SOUL WATCHED THOSE LITTLE FAIRY GIRLS PLAYING, LAUGHING, AND WHATNOT FOR A LONG WHILE. SHE WISHED IN HER VERY OLD AND NOW VERY FORGETFUL MIND THAT SHE COULD BE A YOUNGSTER ONCE AGAIN. THEN, AS SHE WAS THINKING OF HOW SHE WANTED TO BE YOUNG ONCE AGAIN, ONE OF THESE FAIRY GIRLS HAPPENED TO LOOK THE OLD SOUL'S WAY. SHE THEREFORE SAW THE OLD SOUL, RESTING HER VERY WEAKENED OLD BODY, WHICH WAS VERY MUCH IN PAIN AS OFF LATE. THEN THIS FAIRY POINTED HER FINGER TOWARDS HER, THE OLD SOUL, AND TOLD HER PLAYMATES THESE VERY WORDS: "LOOK, THERE IS SOMEONE IN NEED OF OUR HELP". THE CUTE-LOOKING FAIRIES THEN FLEW TO HER RESTING SPOT, AND TOLD THE OLD SOUL THAT THEY WANTED TO HELP HER OUT, BUT ONLY IF IT WAS OKAY BY HER FOR THEM TO HELP HER. THE OLD LADY DID NOT UNDERSTAND WHAT THEY MEANT WHEN THEY TOLD HER THIS, SO SHE PLAYED ALONG WITH THEIR LITTLE GAME, NOT THINKING MUCH,

AND ALL THE WHILE KNOWING VERY WELL WITHIN HER MIND AND SOUL THAT SHE DID NOT HAVE MUCH TO LOSE. SHE MAY, IN FACT, GAIN SOMETHING GOOD FOR HER CURRENT CONDITION THAT SEEMED TO BE CONTROLLED BY THE MANY ACHES AND BODY PAINS THAT SHE WAS IN FACT LIVING WITH DAILY. SHE WAS LIVING OUT HER LAST DAYS OF HER DAILY GIFT OF HER FREE LIFE. AFTER ALL THE AGREEMENTS AND WHATNOT HAD BEEN SETTLED AMONG THESE INDIVIDUALS, THE LITTLE CUTE-LOOKING FAIRIES THEN TOOK OUT A LITTLE BOWL AND FILLED IT UP WITH SOMETHING THAT LOOKED LIKE POWDER. THEY POURED SOME VERY CLEAR LIQUID IN THE BOWL AND MADE SOME SORT OF A POTION IN IT. THEY TOLD THE OLD SOUL TO EAT IT, AND THEN THEY STARTED LAUGHING MERRILY. THEY FLEW AWAY, LEAVING THE POOR OLD SOUL. NOT TOO LONG AFTERWARDS, THIS OLD SOUL DID FEEL VERY DIFFERENT, BODY-WISE. WHEN SHE SAW HER HANDS AND FELT HER FACE, EVERYTHING WAS VERY SMOOTH AND SOFT. THEN THIS OLD SOUL REALIZED AND SAW THE LIGHT THAT YES, SHE WAS YOUNG AGAIN. THIS LADY SOUL, WHO WAS NOW YOUNG AGAIN, LIVED FOR OVER FIFTY MORE YEARS AFTER HER MUCH NEEDED ENCOUNTER WITH THOSE VERY CUTE FAIRY GIRLS, WHOM SHE HAD HAPPENED TO MEET UP WITH ON THAT DAY, WHICH WAS VERY GOOD FOR HER, INDEED.

LAKE HAND

ONE VERY FINE DAY, A YOUNG SLENDER WOMAN SOUL WAS OUT AND ABOUT OUT OF HER VILLAGE, PICKING SOME EDIBLE GREENS FROM THE SOMEWHAT NUMEROUS LAKES SURROUNDING THE AREA CLOSE TO HER VILLAGE. THIS YOUNG WOMAN'S DEAR OLD DAD HAD DIED VERY RECENTLY. THIS WOMAN WAS DOING QUITE WELL ON HER GREENS THAT FATEFUL DAY, AND HER CONTAINER WAS NOW NEARLY FILLED UP WITH THOSE TASTY GREEN PLANTS, WHICH SHE PLANNED TO CHOW DOWN ON WITH HER OTHER FAVORITE FOOD--IN THIS CASE, SEAL OIL. THIS WOMAN SOUL KNEW THAT THE TASTE OF THE COMBINATION OF THE TWO WAS QUITE SATISFING, INDEED. AS THIS LADY WAS COMING TO THIS ONE SMALL LAKE, THIS LIVING SOUL THOUGHT TO HERSELF THAT RESTING A BIT WOULD BE VERY GOOD FOR HER USED-UP ENERGY. SHE ALSO PLANNED TO EAT SOME OF HER FOOD, WHICH SHE HAD TAKEN ALONG, KNOWING BEFOREHAND THAT SHE WOULD GET HUNGRY SOMETIME THAT DAY. AS SHE WAS HAVING HER MUCH NEEDED FOOD, THIS LADY NOTICED A HUMAN HAND OUT IN THE MIDDLE OF THAT SMALL LAKE.

THIS HAND, WITH ITS BODY SUBMERGED, WAS WAVING AT HER. THEN, AFTER IT HAD WAVED AT HER, IT WOULD MAKE SOME SIGNS FOR THIS LADY SOUL TO COME TO IT. THE POOR SOUL DID NOT KNOW WHAT TO DO, NOR DID SHE THINK OF RUNNING AWAY FROM THIS HUMAN HAND, WHICH WAS NOW COMING SLOWLY TOWARDS HER RESTING AREA. ALL THE WHILE, IT WAS WAVING AND USING SIGNS TO BEG HER TO COME TO IT. AS THIS VERY STRANGE HAND GOT CLOSE ENOUGH FOR HER TO SEE WHAT IT REALLY WAS, SHE SAW THAT IT WAS HER VERY MUCH LOVED DEAR OLD DAD, WHO HAD DIED BODILY, VERY RECENTLY, UNDER THAT LAKE. HIS HAND WAS ABOVE THE LAKE WATER, AND HE WANTED HER TO JUMP INTO THAT SMALL LAKE AND JOIN HIM. THIS LADY THEN KNEW WITH ALL HER HEART THAT IF SHE DID, SHE WOULD NO LONGER BE A PART OF THIS WORLD, SO SHE SLOWLY STARTED BACKING OFF, AWAY FROM HER FORMER RESTING SPOT. AS SOON AS IT WAS CLEAR TO HER THAT SHE WAS FAR ENOUGH AWAY, SHE SOMEHOW GOT AND FECT STROWAER. THEREFORE, SHE HEADED BACK TO HER VILLAGE, TAKING STEPS THAT WERE LONGER THAN SHE HAD TAKEN IN HER PAST. THEY WERE ALSO VERY QUICK STEPS, AND WERE CARRIED OUT BY THIS VERY SCARED SOUL AS SHE ESCAPED FROM HER VERY DEAD DAD, WHO WANTED HER TO BE SOMEWHAT REALLY GONE, ALSO.

TRUTH

FOR ANY A LIVING SOUL, THE BELIEF IN VERY EVIL SPIRITS CALLED DEMONS, DEVILS, OR IMPS MAY SOUND FARFETCHED. BUT LET IT NOW BE KNOWN TO ANYONE WHO IS NOT A BELIEVER IN SUCH BAD THINGS THAT THEY ONLY INFLICT HARM, HARDSHIPS, LONELINESS, SADNESS, AND ALL OF THE ONGOING EVILS OCCURRING IN THIS WORLD, BECAUSE THESE ARE ONLY SOME OF THE EFFECTS OF THE ONGOING WORK OF DEMONS. THEY ARE FULL OF ENVY THAT THEY HAD NOT BEEN GIVEN A SECOND CHANCE IN ORDER TO CORRECT THEMSELVES ONCE AGAIN, SO THESE EVIL SPIRITS DO THEIR WORK VERY INVISIBLY, AND CANNOT BE SEEN BY ANYONE ALIVE. IF THE PROBLEMS THEY CREATE FOR ALL SOULS, GOOD AND BAD, WERE SEEN BY ANYONE, NO ONE WOULD WANT TO BE ON THEIR SIDE. THESE VERY EVIL, GROTESQUE CREATURES OF DARKNESS KNOW THAT SOULS DO GO TO A GOOD PLACE CALLED HEAVEN AFTER BODILY DEATH, AND ALSO KNOW THAT THERE IS A PLACE CALLED HELL, WHERE THE SOULS OF FORMER EVIL PEOPLE ARE BEING TORMENTED AND TORTURED UP TO NOW, IN THE CENTER OF THIS EARTH, BY

THESE VERY EVIL CREATURES. SO PLEASE
LISTEN AND HEAR; ALL OF THIS IS VERY TRUE.
IF YOU DO NOT BELIEVE ME, ASK ANY MAN OR
WOMAN WHO DIED PHYSICALLY, BUT SOMEHOW
WAS REVIVED TO BE ALIVE ONCE AGAIN.
THESE LIVING SOULS KNOW THAT THERE IS
CERTAINLY LIFE AFTER DEATH, FOR THE SOUL
OF MAN DOES NOT DIE. THAT IS WHY WE DREAM
AT NIGHT--BECAUSE THE SOUL IS VERY MUCH
ALIVE, EVEN IF THE BODY IS UNCONSCIOUS.
PLEASE DO CARE FOR THE WELL-BEING OF
YOUR FELLOW MAN. REMEMBER, TO BE GOOD
TAKES DAILY PRACTICE, AND IF WORKED ON
DAILY, DESPITE THE MANY SETBACKS, YOU
WILL ONLY GROW AND BLOSSOM. ONLY THEN
WILL YOU KNOW THAT LIKE A BABY, IT NEEDS
NOURISHMENT DAILY. THAT NOURISHMENT
IS ONLY TO STRIVE FOR GOOD, BETTER THAN
BEST. BEWARE DEMONS, AND KNOW, IF YOU
DO NOT FEEL GOOD AT ALL, KNOW THAT THEY
CAN BE BEATEN. THEY ARE NOT INVINCIBLE.
IT IS ONLY UP TO YOU TO FIGHT THEM WITH
GOODNESS. AND JUST KNOW THAT GOOD CAN
WIN OVER EVIL, BUT ALSO KNOW THAT EVIL
WILL NOT VERY EASILY GIVE UP, FOR IT ONLY
WANTS YOUR SOUL, TO TORTURE WITH A
VERY, VERY HOT FIRE SOMEDAY.

SOMEHOW BAD WITHIN

THERE WAS THIS ONE MAN WHO, IN THE EYES OF THE SOULS LIVING AND DOING THEIR DAILY LIVES, ALWAYS HAD SEEMED TO THEM TO BE ONE OF THE ALRIGHT ONES. WHEN HE WOULD GO AROUND HIS VILLAGE, OR WHENEVER HE WAS VISITING OTHER VILLAGES, THEY WOULD ALL SAY THAT HE WAS AN ALRIGHT OLD CHAP. HE HAPPENED TO BE ACTIVE IN THE CHURCH, AND THEREFORE, ALSO WAS A MEMBER OF HIS VILLAGE'S CHOIR GROUP. DURING THE COURSE OF EACH AND EVERY DAY, HE WOULD TEASE AND HAVE HIS SO-CALLED GOOD-NATURED MAN DAYS, FUFILLING THESE THAT WERE MENTIONED ABOVE. ALL THESE WENT ON FOR A VERY LONG PERIOD OF TIME, FOR HE LIVED TO A RIPE OLD AGE, SO TO SAY, UNTIL ONE OF THOSE DAYS THAT HE HAPPENED TO CATCH SOME DISEASE THAT ROBS THE MIND OF ITS CLEAR-THINKING ABILITIES. THAT WAS WHEN THE TRUE COLORS OF THIS MAN STARTED SHOWING UP IN HIS DAILY DYING LIFE. FOR EACH NIGHT, HE WOULD COVER UP THE WINDOWS OF HE AND HIS WIFE'S HOUSE. HE WOULD SIT AT THEIR KITCHEN TABLE WITH A BIG KNIFE, EACH AND EVERY NIGHT. WHEN HIS

WIFE ASKED HIM WHAT WAS GOING ON, HE TOLD HER THAT HE HAD SEEN THE VERY EVIL DEMONS OUTSIDE THEIR WINDOWS, WAITING FOR HIM TO DIE SO THEY COULD TAKE HIS SOUL TO TORTURE HIM WITH THE DEVIL'S FIRE PUNISHMENT FOR ALL HIS FOLLOWERS. HE TOLD HER THAT HE WOULD FIGHT THOSE VERY SCARY-LOOKING DEMONS WAITING OUTSIDE WITH THE BIG KITCHEN KNIFE. FOR SOME REASON NOT KNOWN BY HIS FELLOW VILLAGERS, HE SOMEHOW WAS ONE OF THOSE WITH BAD TASTE AND EVIL THOUGHTS. HE HAD BEEN COVERING THIS UP WITH HIS VERY FAKE GOOD NATURE, BUT SOMEHOW, HE HAD BEEN, IN HIS MIND, A BAD MAN, BUT BEFORE HE DIED, HE WAS VERY RESTLESS, WANTING WATER AND STARTING TO SCREAM AND CRY VERY LOUDLY BEFORE HE DIED.